Literacy at home and school

A GUIDE FOR PARENTS

**Compiled by Vivienne Nicoll
and Lyn Wilkie**

PRIMARY ENGLISH TEACHING ASSOCIATION

Acknowledgments

Our gratitude must go to Wentworth Falls Public School, where our photographs were taken. Particular thanks to librarian Sharon Wilkes, teachers Kerran Michniewica and Robyn Bradley, and the children, all of whom showed great patience. Thanks also to Jozefine Kotze and her son Zachary for their assistance.

National Library of Australia Cataloguing-in-Publication data

Literacy at home and school.

Bibliography
ISBN 0 909955 96 4.
1. Literacy. 2. Reading — Parent participation. 3. Education, Primary — Parent participation. I. Nicoll, Vivienne. II. Wilkie, Lyn. III. Primary English Teaching Association (Australia).

649.58

First published February 1991
Reprinted with minor corrections April 1992
Copyright © Primary English Teaching Association 1991
Laura Street Newtown NSW 2042 Australia
Cover design by Christie & Eckerman
Photographs by Arnold Percy/Blue Mountains Photographics
Edited and designed by Deborah Brown
Typeset in 11/12pt Cheltenham by Tensor Pty Ltd
40-44 Red Lion Street Rozelle NSW 2039
Printed by The Book Printer
83 Longueville Road Lane Cove NSW 2066

FOREWORD

To establish a close, harmonious community of parents, teachers and children — this has been a cherished ideal of the Primary English Teaching Association (PETA) ever since its inception nearly two decades ago.

Over the years, PETA has published many resources for parents, including the 'Suggestions for Parents' columns issued regularly to members as part of the *President's Letter*. International Literacy Year, 1990, seemed the ideal time for the association to build on these suggestions to produce a book wholly concerned with literacy. The aim was to cover the broad issues and answer parents' questions about the teaching of reading and writing in early childhood and the primary years. The book would be written from the twin viewpoints of experience and expertise, by teachers who understand parents' concerns — often because they are parents themselves.

What does the book have to offer?

- There is encouragement and direction for the new parent, for the parent of the preschool child and for the parent of the school pupil. There is accurate information about what happens in classrooms today, and advice for parents who want to support their children's learning at home.
- The teacher will enjoy reading this book because it is full of reassurance and support for what is now happening in so many classrooms in the wake of the 'whole language' revolution.
- From a personal point of view, it has much to offer the grandparent who is given a second chance to play a role in assisting and shaping literacy, without the burden of total responsibility.

This publication is a frank but joyous expression of the strength and power which are created when parents and teachers combine in the education of the child.

Jim Hogan
Publications Director, PETA

February 1991

CONTRIBUTORS

Andrew Buchan is a Vice-President of PETA and Assistant Principal of Enfield Public School, Sydney.

Janis Green is Principal of Toongabbie East Public School, Sydney.

Helen Hogan is a member of the PETA Board and Assistant Principal of Castle Cove Public School, Sydney.

Helen Howard, a former member of the PETA Board, is Principal of Forest Lodge Public School, Sydney.

Lorraine McDonald is current President of PETA, and a Lecturer at the Australian Catholic University, Sydney.

Vivienne Nicoll, a former President of PETA, is currently PETA's Acquisitions Editor.

Richard Parker is PETA's immediate past President, and Director of the Literacy Centre, University of Western Sydney (Macarthur).

Rona Parker formerly lectured at the British Council, Singapore. She currently teaches at Nicholson Street Public School, Sydney.

Victoria Roberts is a former member of the PETA Board, a teacher and a freelance educational consultant.

Mandy Tunica, is a former Vice-President of PETA. She has been a teacher, lecturer, inspector and cluster director, and is now involved in educational consultancy.

Jan Turbill, a former Vice-President of PETA, is a Senior Lecturer at the University of Wollongong.

Ross Weightman, a former member of the PETA Board, is Assistant Principal of Tea Gardens Public School.

Lyn Wilkie has a long association with PETA. She is currently PETA's Company Secretary.

Mary Anne Wilkie teaches at Concord School for Intellectually Impaired Children in Melbourne, Victoria.

CONTENTS

Foreword • *Jim Hogan*   iii
Contributors   iv
Introduction: What is literacy? • *Janis Green*   vii

PART ONE
Before school: The foundations of literacy

1   Babies and books • *Victoria Roberts*   3
2   Reading and writing before school • *Vivienne Nicoll*   7
3   Literacy and the working parent • *Vivienne Nicoll*   12

PART TWO
At school: How do they teach these days?

4   The first years of school • *Helen Howard*   17
5   The teaching of reading • *Richard Parker*   23
6   Any problems? • *Mary Anne Wilkie*   26
7   The teaching of writing: Process writing explained • *Jan Turbill*   29
8   What's all this 'genre' stuff? • *Ross Weightman*   32
9   The teaching of spelling • *Richard Parker*   35
10   Parents in the classroom • *Lorraine McDonald*   39
11   School reports • *Mandy Tunica*   46

PART THREE
At home: Supporting literacy

12   Reading at home • *Vivienne Nicoll*   53
13   Any difficulties? • *Vivienne Nicoll*   58
14   Writing at home • *Helen Hogan*   61
15   Spelling at home • *Rona Parker*   64
16   Homework • *Andrew Buchan*   67
17   Projects • *Andrew Buchan & Helen Hogan*   71
18   Building a family book collection • *Victoria Roberts & Vivienne Nicoll*   77
19   Language learning goes on holiday • *Vivienne Nicoll*   86
20   New Year's resolutions • *Vivienne Nicoll*   89

Glossary • *Ross Weightman*   92
Bibliography • *Vivienne Nicoll*   94

INTRODUCTION
What is literacy?

Janis Green

WHAT DOES IT MEAN TO BE LITERATE?

Is a literate person one who can read, write, spell and use correct grammar and punctuation? A person who is literate may possess these abilities, but literacy involves much more than the use of a set of isolated language skills. Literacy involves the integrated use of listening, thinking, talking, reading and writing in order to:

- communicate with others
- make sense of new situations
- understand new knowledge
- continue to learn throughout life

Literacy is what makes human beings unique in the animal world. Without it, we cannot reach our full potential as people.

Literacy, as the medium for thinking and learning, makes possible the total development of learners of all ages.

Literacy is the ability to manipulate written language, as both a reader and a writer. Reading and writing are the greatest tools of learning that human beings possess and when they are used, with listening, thinking and talking, literacy is in action.

Functional versus enduring literacy

We all know that some people are better readers and writers than others and that some do a lot more reading and writing than others. While some adults read and write only when they have to, others read and write because they want to. They know that reading and writing can bring them pleasure, as well as facilitate further learning.

These two groups of people have achieved different types of literacy. Those who are just literate enough to 'get by', and who will read and write only when required to, have achieved functional literacy — enough literacy to function as human beings. Those who use literacy as a medium of thought and learning have achieved enduring literacy — they are active thinkers and learners. Enduring literates see the value of reading and writing and confidently communicate with others through spoken and written language. They continue to think and learn throughout their lives as they generate ideas, make decisions and critically evaluate all aspects of human existence.

International Literacy Year, 1990, saw worldwide emphasis on increasing the literacy skills of children and adults. In Australia, government funding has enabled special programs to operate for this purpose. The emphasis is not only on making functional literacy available to as many people as possible, but also on guiding more people towards enduring literacy. The achievement of enduring literacy is the ultimate aim of every literacy program.

ASPECTS OF LITERACY

Let us briefly examine the reading, and then the writing, aspects of literacy.

Reading

Reading is a process which enables us to make sense of print. When we read, we use what we already know, combined with the print we see, to make sense of what we read. Reading is about making meaning. It is not about stumbling over each word and 'sounding it out' to get it right. Reading does not occur unless the reader understands what has been read.

Readers comprehend the meaning that someone else has written. Effective readers focus on meaning. Their mistakes usually don't cause serious loss of meaning and they are able to correct any that do. As they read, they continually predict what will come next. They are able to predict by calling on their prior knowledge of the subject matter as well as on their knowledge of how written language flows. They do not try to 'sound out' unknown words but they may use their knowledge of letters and their 'sounds' to check their predictions. They have a positive attitude towards books and reading and they approach reading tasks with the expectation that they will succeed.

Writing

Writing is a process which enables us to compose our own meaning, usually for others to read. It can involve thinking, feeling, talking and reading as well as writing.

Through writing we learn how to use its conventions of spelling, grammar, punctuation and handwriting. These conventions are part of writing. They have no meaning as isolated skills — their purpose is to serve writing so that others will be able to read it. Beginning writers need time to concentrate on what they want to say, rather than on the correctness of conventions. Mastery of the conventions will develop, with guidance, in the meaningful context of children's own writing.

Writers express their meanings for others to read. Effective writers are confident about their ability to write and they know that writing is useful to them. They are prepared to 'have a go' at using the conventions as they concentrate on putting ideas on paper. The more they write, the more they increase their control over the conventions of writing and over different forms of writing. They are able to organise their writing, revise it and edit it, before making decisions about publishing it. They know why they are writing and they know who will read what they have written.

THE BEGINNINGS OF LITERACY

Literacy learning begins at birth. In the years before school, parents play a vital role as their children's first literacy teachers. Consider all the things that children learn before school as they associate with others, observe what others do and try to do the same things. This learning happens naturally, in a social context, and is controlled by each learner as he or she decides what to attempt next. Children appear to learn to talk with much less effort than they need when they are learning to read and write.

Listening and talking

Listening and talking are the beginnings of literacy learning. Children learn to talk because they want to be like others around them and they realise that through talk they will be able to express their needs. Learning to talk has a purpose for them and each time they attempt to communicate they are encouraged by the smiles, attention and verbal responses they receive from those around them. They are not criticised if they make mistakes. They are assisted in a collaborative way as those who converse with them repeat their words, build on them, and demonstrate correct pronunciation and sentence structure.

Children are encouraged to experiment with language as they take part in normal family routines. Their learning is continuous and much of it occurs incidentally.

Reading and writing

Children who see people reading and writing in the home naturally wish to do the same things themselves. They pretend to read and write because they see that older people have reasons to do this. Children's first attempts to join in the reading of stories, or to tell their own versions, are the beginnings of reading development, just as their first crayon marks on paper are the beginning of writing development.

As they experiment with reading and writing, children need the same kind of positive encouragement and support as they receive when they experiment with talking. From such beginnings, interest in reading and writing develops, and skills are gradually mastered, as learners are able to collaborate with experienced readers and writers. It is this collaborative learning, during which adults totally support inexperienced learners by building on present understandings and by making them aware of what they do know, that has the greatest influence on future literacy attitudes. Children can only learn about reading and writing if they actually try to read and write, just as they learn about talking by experimenting with words.

HOW DOES LITERACY DEVELOP?

Literacy develops as children experience reading and writing, in different ways and for different purposes. Literacy learning is possible when children are able to use what they already know to help them make sense of whatever is presented as new knowledge or a new skill. It does not happen simply because a teacher or parent passes on information and gives learners plenty of practice with new 'skills'. Literacy learning depends on understanding, not on the practice of skills out of context. Individual learners have to take new knowledge about reading and writing, add it to what they already know, and construct understanding in their own way.

Literacy learning becomes difficult for children when teachers and parents forget that their own understandings, based on years of learning and maturity, are very different from the understandings of much less experienced learners. The difference between beginning or developing literates and adult, independent literates is the amount of known information to be called upon to foster new understandings and knowledge.

HELPING CHILDREN TOWARDS LITERACY

Children enter school with very different knowledge about what literacy is and very different reading and writing abilities. The child who can read independently and the child who cannot read, but can turn the pages of a book and make up a story, both know something about reading. The child who can write a correctly formed sentence and the child who can put squiggles or random letters on a page both know something about writing.

It is the ability to recognise what each child already knows, and to guide literacy learning by building on this at appropriate times, that is the greatest challenge to teachers and parents as they support developing literacy learners. Throughout the school years, parents and teachers should work in partnership to provide support for developing readers and writers.

Literacy learning is a social experience because it depends on demonstrations from, collaboration with, and continuous feedback and response from, other people. It happens, at home and at school, when children:
- are surrounded by people who listen, talk, think, read and write
- can see purposes for reading and writing
- share experiences (a picnic, a visit to the zoo) which are then talked about at home
- share books (especially stories) and talk about them with more experienced readers
- have plenty of books to handle and read
- see print all around them
- have models of how people read and write
- have opportunities to read and write
- know that people expect them to read and write
- are given choices about what they read and write
- feel free to 'have a go' at reading and writing (including spelling)
- are able to talk about their reading and writing
- experience feelings of success
- feel responsible for their own reading and writing
- have confidence in their own ability
- understand what reading, writing and learning can do for them

Let us strive together, parents and teachers, to develop a partnership which will support our literacy learners and ensure that they have a future as enduring literates who will continue to use reading and writing to learn throughout their lives.

PART ONE

BEFORE SCHOOL
The foundations of literacy

CHAPTER 1
Babies and books

Victoria Roberts

READING WITH THEA

The first haircut, a new tooth and a bruise on the face from falling over in the bath
— quite a day! Today has been just one of the memorable and exciting days of the
last year, and at moments like this when I have the luxury of sitting and reflecting
on my new life as a mum I wonder how I finally reached the point where I can chuckle.
So much of it has been trying and I have felt so inexperienced and definitely not in
control. It has proved to be the busiest, the most frustrating and yet probably the most
rewarding year of my teaching career. It began on Sunday, 20 April, when Thea Emily
was born. She came in a big hurry and she has been in a big hurry ever since. She
is so independent and impatient.

In typical, professional teacher fashion I had inserviced myself and was going to
do all the 'right' things with Thea. We read to her in the delivery suite as soon as
she was born. James held her and I launched into Aliki's *Welcome, Little Baby*. It was
a big success: she promptly fell asleep. For the first week or so of her life we read
this book hundreds of times in the vain hope that she would go to sleep again, but
oh no — we had not been blessed with a sleeper. It was time to experiment with other
books.

Tomie de Paola's *Mother Goose* became a favourite for all three of us. James and
I took it in turns to sit in the rocking chair and read nursery rhymes. It must have
had some effect because she still likes them, especially loud, robust ones like 'The
Grand Old Duke of York' and 'This Is the Way the Ladies Ride'.

BOOKS AS PLAYTHINGS

I had read Margaret Meek's *Learning to Read* and I was determined that my child would
see books and reading as being an important part of play. So, despite Dorothy Butler's
hesitancy about cloth and board books, Thea has had plenty of these to play with.
They are kept with her toys and she pulls them out, drags them around and hoys them
just as she does with her rattles, blocks and Duplo. Occasionally we find her sitting
underneath a table turning the pages and talking to herself. (We hope this is the
beginning of reading-like behaviour.)

She already has a definite favourite, Fiona Pragoff's *Growing*. This hard card book has beautiful photos of babies with one word of text to accompany each photo, for example *crawling, sitting, splashing*. Thea talks to the babies in the book in the same way that she talks to herself in the mirror. This book has rescued us many a time on a long car trip or in the doctor's waiting room or in the supermarket queue . . .

SOME PROBLEMS

We try to read to Thea at least once each day. This is becoming harder now that she is mobile because she crawls off in the middle of the story or wants to take hold of the book herself. I have failed to get Thea so hooked on books that she doesn't move, like Raja in David Doake's *Reading Begins at Birth*. I just keep reading and hope that she will come crawling back.

The other problem is that we have not been particularly successful at teaching Thea the difference between the paper books that we want to keep intact and her play books that we have allowed her to put in her mouth. We keep the 'reading' books on the shelf, out of reach between two lovely elephant bookends, and she knows that they are special because she wants to get at them. We'll persevere because as a teacher I always used to say that I didn't want books that were in pristine condition; I wanted books-that were read and loved. Well, we will certainly know which ones are loved!

Our house is full of books and there is hardly a room where Thea can't find a book, but this is rapidly changing because Thea has a fascination for title pages. Now the study door is closed and we cannot leave books beside our bed or on the coffee table. If we forget, woe betide us — when we return the title page will be gone! Some we have rescued in time to resurrect with sticky tape. Others she has eaten. (You'll be pleased to know, I'm sure, that paper comes out the other end in the same size pieces that it went in the mouth. Just another one of the wonderful things I've learnt this year!)

CHEAP 'BOOKS'

Paper with print has always fascinated Thea. From as young as five weeks she has very intently watched James turn the pages of the newspaper. The first thing she reached out for was the newspaper, and she thinks all the inserts in the newspaper are hers. Too bad if you thought you might like to browse through that special catalogue! We once contemplated a 'No unsolicited mail' sticker for our letterbox, but we've put that idea on hold until Thea no longer has a yen for advertising brochures and the like. They are cheap reading material and more easily surrendered than title pages.

EXPECTATIONS...VERSUS REALITY

I may have read all the right books, but, as my mother says, Thea has not and she seems determined not to conform. Not only does she not sleep a great deal; she weaned herself, got her top teeth before the bottom teeth and embarrassed me at the Early Childhood Centre when we went for the first major screening. The Sister wanted Thea to reach out and take a rattle and she would not. The Sister wrote on the form that Thea couldn't do that and Thea promptly reached out and took the form she was writing on. I tried to explain that she had tested Thea using the wrong item, but the test said *rattle*, not *paper*. Did Thea fail the test?

I have learnt so much about expectations. I've spent the last few years inservicing teachers and reassuring them that there is no 'right' or 'wrong' order to teach language skills; that each child in the class will not necessarily do the same thing at the same time or age as another; that each child is an individual with different needs and learning styles. And yet in the last nine months I've done everything I've told teachers not to do. I've compared Thea with the other babies in my mothers' group. I've worried about what she can't do. And here I am writing about my worry that I haven't been able to make Thea into the 'ideal reading child' that I read about in Dorothy Butler's and David Doake's books.

What am I going to do about it?

I'm going to keep reading to her. I'm going to continue sharing books with her and letting her choose what we read, even if I do have to keep reading Anthony Browne's *I Like Books*, Rod Campbell's *Noisy Book* and Anthea Sieveking's *The Baby's Book of Babies* to the exclusion of other books which have a story. And no doubt James will continue to read Jan Ormerod's *Dad and Me Reading* and Carol Jones's *Old Macdonald Had a Farm*, because Thea has given up on me with these ones. I say, 'Go and ask Dad' and she crawls off or screams. I'm going to continue introducing new books which have a story rather than being collections of words, and I'm going to persevere with the Ahlbergs' *Peepo!* and *The Baby's Catalogue*, which to date have been unsuccessful. I might be brave and reintroduce some books that have already lost their title pages, like *Animals Should Definitely Not Wear Clothing* and *This Little Puffin*. And I'm going back to school. I'm going to teach Year 1 two days a week, so I'll be busy: too busy to spend too much time worrying about what Thea isn't doing yet; too busy worrying about putting my teaching ideals into practice in the classroom for the first time in a long while.

Of course I'll revisit *Babies Need Books* and *The Read-Aloud Handbook*, and I'll reread the chapters for the next age group (9-12 months) in *Baby Games* and *Play and Learn*, but in the meantime I'll just keep loving Thea and rest assured that we chose the right name, because she certainly is a divine gift!

If, like me, you have a child and the best of intentions, the books listed below may be useful. But remember, your child may have very strong ideas of her own — especially if she's anything like you!

SOME BOOKS FOR YOU

Here are some reference books that I have found helpful.

Tony Bradman, *Will You Read to Me?*, Thorsons, 1986.
Dorothy Butler, *Cushla and Her Books*, Hodder & Stoughton, 1975.
Dorothy Butler, *Babies Need Books*, Penguin Books, 1988.
David B. Doake, *Reading Begins at Birth*, Scholastic, 1988.
Carolyn Buhai Haas, *Look at Me: Creative Learning Activities for Babies and Toddlers*, Chicago Review Press, 1987.
Maggie Jones, *Play and Learn*, Conran Octopus, 1989.
Elaine Martin, *Baby Games: The Joyful Guide to Child's Play from Birth to Three Years*, Millenium, 1988.

Margaret Meek, *Learning to Read*, Bodley Head, 1982.
Jim Trelease, *The Read-Aloud Handbook*, Penguin Books, 1986.

SOME BOOKS FOR YOUR CHILD

Some of our favourite books for sharing together are also listed here. Those marked with an asterisk have photos rather than illustrations. (Thea seems to like photos, especially ones of babies, cats and dogs.)

Janet & Allan Ahlberg, *The Baby's Catalogue*, Picture Puffin, Penguin Books.
Janet & Allan Ahlberg, *Peepo!*, Picture Puffin, Penguin Books.
Aliki, *Welcome, Little Baby*, Piper.
Mitsumasa Anno, *Peekaboo!*, Bodley Head.
Judi & Ron Barrett, *Animals Should Definitely Not Wear Clothing*, Kay & Ward.
Marc Brown, *Hand Rhymes*, Collins.
Marc Brown, *Play Rhymes*, Collins.
Anthony Browne, *I Like Books*, Julia MacRae.
Anthony Browne, *Things I Like*, Julia MacRae.
Rod Campbell, *Noisy Book*, Lothian.
Tomie de Paola, *Tomie de Paola's Mother Goose*, Methuen.
Bill Gillham, *And So Can I!*, Magnet.*
Carol Jones, *Old Macdonald Had a Farm*, Angus & Robertson.
Elizabeth Matterson, *This Little Puffin: Finger Plays and Nursery Games*, Puffin, Penguin Books.
Nanette Newman, *Bad Baby*, Collins.
Jan Ormerod, *Dad and Me Reading*, Walker Books.
Fiona Praggof, *Growing*, Gollancz.*
Jack Prelutsky & Marc Brown, *The Walker Book of Read Aloud Rhymes for the Very Young*, Walker Books.
Anthea Sieveking, *The Baby's Book of Babies*, Collins.*
Anthea Sieveking, *What's Inside?*, Collins.*
Shigeo Watanabe, *Hallo! How Are You?*, Picture Puffin, Penguin Books.
Harriet Ziefert & Emilie Boon, *Daddy, Can You Play with Me?*, Picture Puffin, Penguin Books.

CHAPTER 2
Reading and writing before school

Vivienne Nicoll

From birth to the age of five, children can learn invaluable lessons about literacy. They can learn many of the purposes for which the community finds reading and writing useful, and especially how much pleasure there is to be found in storybook reading. They can learn about the way we use print in our society, and begin to experiment with 'writing' for themselves.

Learning to read and write begins at home — not with flashcards, drills or special kits, but with pleasurable, purposeful, everyday involvement with print. Parents are the key to this learning. You can help by providing your children with books, paper and writing utensils, and by finding the time and enthusiasm to share reading and writing with them. Involvement with reading teaches children lessons about writing; as they experiment with writing, they learn lessons about reading.

READING BEFORE SCHOOL

Begin with stories

Children can enjoy the pleasure of stories from a very early age. In fact, many parents begin reading to their children at birth or in the first six months of life. Share simple picture-storybooks with your child whenever you can — at bedtime and at other times when you both deserve a quiet break from the bustle of work and play. We know that time spent in 'lap-reading' is invaluable in developing in children a love of stories. (For suggestions of books to begin with, see chapter 18, 'Building a family book collection'.)

Storytime teaches other lessons, too: about how different written language sounds to the language of speech and about the way books work. We adults may take it for granted that in English you begin to read books at the front, not the back, and that the words run from top to bottom and left to right; or that the words of a story say the same thing every time. But for children these are new and important concepts that are only learnt through sharing books with an experienced adult.

Sharing doesn't just involve *reading* to children. Take time to *chat* about the pictures and story so far, and to relate characters and plot to people and events in the child's own world. Listen and respond to children's comments about the book. Encourage their questions about the book and ask thoughtful questions yourself. In particular, invite them occasionally to predict what might happen next in the story.

Reread old favourites

Don't be surprised if your children want you to read their favourite books again and again. You'll find it helps them learn the 'tunes' of written language, as well as extending their vocabulary. Encourage youngsters to join in with a repetitive chorus, to speak the words of the characters and to say familiar parts of the text with you. From time to time make a game of taking turns to *retell* a familiar story.

When children sit alone turning the pages of a book and telling themselves the story, or when they 'read' an old favourite to Teddy or Dolly, they are exhibiting 'reading-like behaviour' — a fancy term which means that they are learning about stories and their importance.

When children begin to show an interest in print, run your fingers lightly under the words as you read. This will highlight the relationship between stories, print and reading. Encourage your youngsters sometimes to hold the book and turn the pages for themselves. Make time available as part of the bedtime-story ritual for children to look through their favourites before lights-out. A reading lamp and a bedside table are two gifts which will assist children to develop as independent readers long before they can actually recognise the words on a page.

As toddlers turn into preschoolers, extend your sharing of stories through creative activities: simply made finger puppets could tell the story to each other; you can make models from playdough; or paint a scene from the story.

Make yours a reading home

Actions speak louder than words. Show your children you value reading by providing a good model of reading yourself. Preschoolers learn much about the reasons for reading as they observe other family members enjoying books, magazines and newspapers or using them as sources of information. You can demonstrate and share the importance of reading in all aspects of your everyday life: cooking, fixing things, gardening, work, study, hobbies.

Your young child's room can be an environment which fosters reading — decorate it with posters and mobiles, add a noticeboard with a changing display, and provide a bookshelf at child-height for easy access. Write out nursery rhymes or simple poems on large sheets of paper to stick on the walls, and chant or sing them as you dress the toddler for play. The rhythm, rhyme and repetition of nursery rhymes teach children much about how language works.

Give books as presents. Remember how special *you* found those first books you received as Christmas or birthday gifts? Choose information books, fairytale and nursery-rhyme collections, picture-storybooks, longer books with short chapters and, of course, collections of poetry for children. Visit the local bookshop together as a regular outing — a paperback book is a better and more lasting buy than a cheap toy or a swag of lollies.

Enrol your young children as members of their local library. It's important to introduce them to a variety of authors and illustrators early on. Through your shared visits you will help your children to see that books are important, and to develop an understanding of how to go about selecting books for themselves.

Don't forget about the world of print outside books — involve your children in 'reading' labels on jars, bottles and packets, the family letters and cards you receive, street signs, television advertisements, and all the other print to be found around and outside the home. Draw children's attention to the role which print plays in daily life: in the shops, on the street, on television and so on.

Reading is fun

Above all, don't make the sharing of books a chore. Your own enthusiasm for a story, as shown in your laughter, tears or wonder, and your own ability to make the language of books come alive as you read stories and poems and nursery rhymes, will do much to make your children avid readers!

WRITING AT HOME

Writing plays an important (though often seemingly invisible) role in almost every home. Parents and older siblings leave scribbled messages for each other, note forthcoming events on an engagement calendar and write lists of jobs to be done or purchases to be made. Greetings are written on cards, cheques are written, notes are sent to school, and various forms are filled out.

On top of all this, in some homes writing is used for work and study tasks in taking notes and composing essays and reports. For some families a typewriter or a home computer with word-processing program are indispensable technology.

Sharing family experiences of writing with children lays the foundations for writing in school and beyond. Writing, like reading, should be part of the home environment and should be shared as often as possible.

Sharing involvement

The first step is to *show* children how you use writing. Begin by allowing them to see you writing — be it the shopping list, greeting cards, inscribing names on belongings, or dashing off a note to stick on the family message board or the fridge. As children begin to show interest in what you're doing, involve them in thinking of things to put on the shopping list or in sending a greeting in the letter you're writing to Gran.

As soon as youngsters seem able to hold a writing implement, provide them with an ever-widening variety of writing materials. You may start with scrap paper and chubby crayons and move next to textas, pens and pencils and different sorts of paper — lined, plain, coloured, in sheets or booklets. A sturdy, easel-type blackboard and chalks make a terrific gift at the age of about two or three, as do magnetic letters for use on the board or fridge.

At first children are content to draw and write wherever they are, but from three years old it is a good idea to provide their own special place where they can draw or 'write' uninterrupted. Children who have a small table or desk and a chair, and a supply of different sorts of paper, seem less likely to scribble on walls, tablecloths, library books and so on! It is a shame ever to discourage children's impulse to write and draw, so try to find some 'non-taboo' areas for such activity. For example, given a little good humour and a hose, you may be able to tolerate your youngsters drawing with chalks on the backyard wall or paving, or the driveway.

Enjoy your children's early attempts at drawing and writing. Find a place to display their efforts, on a kitchen noticeboard or the fridge. A display board in the child's bedroom is another good idea.

When children reach the preschool years (three to four), you can introduce writing as part of their imaginative play. 'Letters' can be written to relatives and friends, then 'posted'. 'Shopping lists' can be drawn up and used, and products in the child's make-believe shop can be labelled.

The point to remember is that when adults write, we do it for a real purpose within the context of our daily lives, and so it should be when we introduce our children to print — all uses of writing should be for a purpose meaningful to the child.

Names, letters, words

Find ways for children to see their names written down: on a nameplate for the bedroom door; written with textas on their drawings and displayed on the fridge or noticeboard; on various belongings; as part of the family greeting on cards and letters. You will be surprised how quickly children learn to recognise their name and begin attempting to write it.

Many three and four year olds are curious about the alphabet. Some have already enjoyed many experiences with it, perhaps actively from sitting and experimenting at a typewriter or word processor with a parent whose work they have interrupted, or perhaps more passively from their viewing of 'Sesame Street'.

Once they have shown an interest, encourage it. You can safely call the letters by their *names* — not their 'sounds'. (For example say 'bee', not 'buh', for the letter *b*.) Borrow alphabet books from the library to share, and talk about each letter and all the objects drawn to illustrate it. Provide an icecream container of plastic or foam letters, both capitals and lower-case. Make these readily available on the toy shelf and encourage free play with them — children soon lose interest if you take the initiative from them. When your involvement in the play is welcomed, bring the letters together into words, starting perhaps with the names of family, friends and loved objects.

In time, children will begin to experiment with bringing the letters together to copy words in their environment. Magnetic letters and an appropriate surface (fridge door or blackboard) are a must for this activity. Children will soon begin to experiment with individual letters and groups of them as part of their own writing on paper.

Once children have displayed this interest in writing (usually some time in their fourth year), do your best to help them write whenever they ask. If they have seen others use writing in the home, and if parents have involved them in purposeful writing as part of daily family life, children will begin to 'write' for their own purposes: practising writing their own name on paintings and drawings, writing greetings or messages, even 'writing' something on the word processor and printing it out to share later. Most importantly, respond positively and seriously to the message and intent of your child's writing.

If you have the time, you'll find a myriad of ways to make your home an actively literate one.

Write simple, funny captions for the photograph album.

Make family scrapbooks of holidays and other major events.

School-age children may enjoy writing and illustrating stories for their preschool brothers or sisters, or cutting out magazine pictures and turning them into an alphabet book. These homemade books can be stapled or sewn into sturdy, coloured covers and will soon become special favourites.

IN CONCLUSION

Reading and writing are complex cultural activities. For all of us, reading and writing are learnt culturally as we use print purposefully in our dealings with family, friends and the immediate community. We do not need kits, activity sheets or endless drills to prepare children well for literacy learning at school. The best start we can give children is to make them welcome as eager apprentices to our own reading and writing practices.

Eleni says her message to Nanna reads: 'Thanks for taking me to the zoo, Nanna'.

CHAPTER 3
Literacy and the working parent

Vivienne Nicoll

THE BURDEN OF GUILT

When working parents need or choose to put their infants into child-care, they often experience bouts of guilt. I know that I have. My four-year-old son is developing well and has been with excellent, loving and stable caregivers since he was nine months old, but I can always find reasons to worry that he has missed out on certain valuable experiences because he has not been with me all day, every day.

True, I don't cook gingerbread people with him and we've never been to playgroup or the swimming pool together. I know, however, that my son is in a happier home because his mother enjoys her work (and needs the income!) and I still marvel at how much his social skills have grown during his time in a long-daycare centre.

Guides for parents (like this one) can add to the working parent's feelings of guilt. They often assume an ideal world in which parents and children have unlimited time together. Some leave you asking questions such as, 'Will my child be illiterate because I haven't been home to read to him ten times a day?'. Of course not. But working parents do have to plan carefully and find 'quality' time to share language and literacy experiences with the baby, toddler or preschooler.

HOW TO SPEND QUALITY TIME WITH YOUR CHILD

Here are some ideas you might try. With some trial, effort and good humour, they have worked for our family.
- If your child is in a child-care centre, you can usually observe whether the program provides experiences with books and writing. If not, remember that most centres have active parent committees and are happy for you to suggest ideas, or to raise funds for extra storybooks, blackboards, crayons and so on.
- When you pick up your child after work, try to find out from the adult caregivers as much as you can about the highlights of your child's day. Were there any special events or memorable happenings? Did they use playdough or do finger-painting? Finding out such little things gives you a common experience to *talk about* with your child on the way home and in the precious moments you have together in the evening.
- Find out from the caregivers what songs and rhymes your child is currently singing or chanting. Your child's language development, as well as your relationship,

will be enhanced if you can share these songs and nursery rhymes. Purchase a good nursery-rhyme treasury (see chapter 18) if you aren't an expert on the words of these. Another good reference we've found helpful is *The Useful Book: songs and ideas from Play School,* published and marketed by the ABC.

● If, because of care arrangements, your child misses out on television programs such as 'Play School', watch videotapes of them together later — on weekends, in the early evening, whenever you can. You can buy the 'Play School' videos from the ABC.

● If you drive together to and from child-care, use this time to sing songs, chant rhymes or listen to cassettes on the car stereo. I found the 'Play School' cassettes invaluable. Even in my previous car, which had no radio or stereo, we would spend an hour a day singing, and even doing finger plays (easy in peak-hour traffic when the car is so often at a standstill, provided that you can cope with the funny looks from other motorists!).

● One major decision that my husband and I had to face early on was how to make the most of our limited time at home with Craig. After work, there is always a dilemma — do you get the household chores done or do you abandon them to spend uninterrupted time with your child? We have found, unfortunately, that many chores have to wait until after our son has gone to bed so that one of us at least can be totally involved with him. So one of us cooks dinner while the other spends time with Craig. In this way we can provide the kinds of literacy experiences mentioned in chapter 2 of this book.

● On weekdays, we've found that the best time for storybook reading is after Craig's bath. Sometimes he sits on my lap on the lounge, sometimes we cuddle up on his bed or the 'big bed' to read. It's a very special time to be together, and we'll often get through six or seven books.

● On weekends, we try to spend one day catching up. Maybe the three of us will squeeze into the big bed to read our books. After Saturday breakfast, out comes the board and together we'll draw, scribble or play with the magnetic letters. (While we don't really think 'Sesame Street' is a wonderful program, we must say it has given Craig a great interest in and knowledge of the alphabet, which will help him when he first attempts to write.)

● If your job involves literacy in any way, try to make this part of your child's experience. An occasional trip to 'Mummy's office' or 'the hospital' (Daddy's workplace) has not only helped our child build a sense of self, but has also shown him the value of the things we do with print. I often have to read or write for work purposes at the dining room table, and now Craig will get his paper and textas and come and 'work' with me. He is fascinated by my computer and word-processing program, and so I have a 'Craig' file just for him. It's worth shelving work for half an hour to see the delight he finds in 'writing' for himself. Each time we use the computer together, I write a sentence about something he has done that day and print it out — he loves 'reading' it to other people.

● It requires effort, but *sometimes* at weekends I try to provide the literacy experiences that some other parents provide on weekdays — cooking from a recipe, going to the library or bookshop, taking the time during supermarket shopping to 'read' the labels. I guess the difference for the working parent is that you have to consciously *choose* to do these things instead of something you'd rather do for yourself.

DON'T LET IT GET YOU DOWN!

My advice is not to let guilt get to you — easy to say, but difficult to do! When I first went back to work, every evening I would try to pack into two hours of little Craig's life all the things I thought should be happening: singing, reading, clapping games, playing with puzzles or Duplo. But something was wrong . . . neither of us was really *enjoying* it.

It took me a while to learn to relax and take my lead from him. So what if we haven't shared a storybook for two nights in a row? Tomorrow night we'll probably read *The Three Little Pigs* six times, along with four or five other books — and we'll have fun!

PART TWO

AT SCHOOL
How do they teach these days?

CHAPTER 4
The first years of school

Helen Howard

Schools have changed — not only since you and I were kids, but even since I started teaching. Little wonder, then, that parents feel the need to ask questions about those first years of school — about what the school does and how they can help their children.

One of the most significant changes in education is the recognition of parents' role in their children's education. Gone are the days when parents were made to feel that the school knew it all, that they must look to the teachers for any knowledge of how children learn. Gone are the days when any child who came to school able to read and write had to be retaught the school's way, the *correct* way. Instead there is an understanding that parents and teachers are partners. As children's first educators, parents teach them many significant things; and if we as teachers can replicate the teaching style of parents in those early years, children may learn at school as easily and naturally as they did then.

Another thing that has changed is the teaching of literacy. Where once reading, writing and spelling were taught as separate subjects, with a 'skills and drills' mentality, nowadays we recognise that talking, reading, writing and spelling are all interrelated, and should be taught as a whole.

TALKING

A head start

The greatest gift parents can give children is to send them off to school with good oral language. Children who are used to talking, being listened to, having their questions answered and being told new things will have an advantage. Most teachers believe that the best talkers will also be the best readers and writers.

Teaching a child to talk takes patience. Children learn by practising, playing with language, asking questions and pointing out everything they know. It can be trying to answer their eternal questions, but this is where learning begins. I once overheard a mother answering her two year old's question 'Is that a tree?' with 'I already told you it was'. Compare this answer: 'Yes, it's a tree. It's a big tree, isn't it? It has a lot of leaves on it. Can you hear the sound of the wind in the leaves? I wonder if there are any birds in the tree?'

Children ask lots of questions, but have you ever thought about the types of questions you ask them? Try to ask questions which require more than a yes or no answer. Ask questions which make your child think: 'Why do you think so-and-so happened?' Don't provide the answer too quickly — give them the means for them to find it for themselves.

Some of the best development in learning to talk occurs when child and parent talk about a shared experience: cooking a cake, visiting the fire station, even watching a television program together. As you recall what happened, there are many opportunities for you to ask probing questions and to elaborate upon your child's comments.

Talking in school

When children come to school, oral language will still be an important part of the school day: during show and tell, news time, imaginative play, small group and paired activities, as well as more formal whole class discussions in which children learn to take turns.

From spoken to written language: bridging the gap

At school, children will need to be aware of two different types of language:
• everyday language, which is constantly built up as parents and children listen, answer questions, discuss and investigate together
• book language, which children only learn from having books read to them over and over again

Book language does differ from speech, both in vocabulary and structure. As children start to read, the knowledge of how language is structured in books helps them to predict unknown words.

How can you help at home?
• Read to children every night, if you can. Encourage and respond to your child's spontaneous comments as you read.
• When you read, respond to the text — wonder out loud, ask your child to think what might happen, explore the illustrations together.
• Teach them songs and rhymes. Children need and love the repetition of songs, rhymes and chants, where everything is repeated, practised and played with over and over again.

READING AND WRITING

All children are different

One of the most important things children achieve before school is learning to talk, and one of the most important things they will achieve at school is learning to read and write. It takes most children approximately eighteen months to learn to talk, and about the same time to learn to read and write. Not all children are the same, however. Some start to talk early, some late; some walk early, some late. So it is with reading and writing. Some can do both before starting school, while others don't take off until about eighteen months or two years later.

The chances are that your children already understand a lot about books when they come to school. Do they make up stories from books as they pretend to read? Do they complain if you leave out a page when you read the bedtime story?

Some children will come to school still thinking that the message comes from the picture; others knowing that it comes from the print, but not yet realising that the message is always the same, however many times you read it.

On the other hand, some children will already be able to read and write, as they have taught themselves. These children should not be held back, but praised for their efforts. The teacher will know which books are most suitable to give these children practice and may send them home each night with a little book to read to you. These children need books at two levels: challenging books when the teacher is there to guide and assist; and easy books for showing off at home or quiet reading in class, to practise new reading strategies.

WHAT WILL THEY LEARN AT SCHOOL?

Whatever level children have reached, these are the important things they will learn about reading in kindergarten:

- books are fun
- books carry messages
- it is the print that carries the message
- the message is unchanging and can be read back
- direction is important to reading — in English, from left to right, top to bottom
- there is an exact match between the spoken and written word
- books have their own language and say things in a particular way which differs from talk

As preschoolers, children are interested in and encouraged to observe everything. Now we want them to focus on the finer details of pictures and especially of print. From the first day of school we focus on print, in three ways: by focusing on the print in books, by focusing on the print written by the teacher, and by focusing on the print children write themselves.

Focusing on the print in books

Each day the teacher will read to the class from a Big Book. This is a very large book with large print which the whole class can see as they sit on the carpet at the teacher's feet. (The idea is that just as parents read favourite bedtime stories to their children, so too can teachers read favourite books in such a way that all the children are able to see the print and the pictures.)

As the teacher reads she or he points to each word so that children begin to realise that there is a perfect match between the spoken word and the written word, and that print is read from left to right, top to bottom.

How can you help at home?
- Do praise your child's efforts.

- Trace the print with your finger as you read.
- Do assist with unfamiliar words, but give children a chance to track back through their memory first.
- Don't accuse them of reading from memory (or allow your friends to). It is all part of the process. Keep thinking back to when they were learning to talk and note the similarities.
- Remember, reading is not simply about knowing the words — it is also about stopping and discussing what happened, why it happened and what might happen next, and talking about the illustrations.

Focusing on the print written by the teacher

Each day the teacher will select items of news told by the children and write them down. The children watch their messages being written, then read them with the teacher's assistance. They can predict what the words will be because it is their spoken language which has been written down. This process teaches children that a message can be written down and that it can be read back.

How can you help at home?
- Let your child see you writing.
- Write messages and read them together.
- Write down stories or messages as your child dictates to you, then read them back together.

Focusing on the print children write themselves

From their first day at school your children will be encouraged to write. Many will begin by writing letters — capitals and lower-case — scattered all over the page. This will gradually change as their understanding develops: upper-case letters will give way to lower-case, as this is the emphasis at school; they will write across the page, sometimes putting a full stop at the end of each line; and finally they will produce row after row of letters fluently.

Often teachers will encourage children to draw before they write: this helps them assemble their thoughts and gives them a point of reference for their writing. When asked what their writing says, they may answer, 'I don't know — you read it to me', or they may make up a very detailed story (to accompany a picture more than the writing) which may change on every telling.

When children come to school able to write their own name and the letters of the alphabet, it is usually in capital letters. Teachers may complain about this. It is sometimes difficult to convince young children that small letters are used at school — they may think the teacher is saying that Mum or Dad is wrong.

There are two good reasons for insisting on lower-case letters: first, because this is how books are usually printed; and second, because from the first day of kindergarten we are aiming to establish the foundations for cursive writing — training children in correct letter formation, pencil grip, size and slope of letters — so that later they need only add the hooks to have cursive writing.

How can you help at home?
- Buy alphabet books as well as storybooks, especially those which feature lower-case as well as upper-case letters.
- Make words with plastic and magnetic letters.
- Encourage children to use lower-case letters, with capitals where appropriate.
- Let them help you with the shopping list.
- Invite them to add notes to letters or cards.
- Write messages to each other as part of your family routine.
- Respond to their letters to you.

Spelling

When parents teach their children to write the letters of the alphabet they often teach the letter names to match. As children learn to read and write they learn to associate the letter name with the sound it represents in a word. This becomes a vital first step in the spelling process as children write the sounds they hear in words.

You will hear the term *invented* (or *approximated*) spelling. Just as children approximate adult speech when learning to talk, so too they need to be able to approximate the adult version when learning to read, write and spell. Their invented spelling will grow closer and closer to the standard form as they progress, through levels which include:
- lines of scribble
- a line of letters which are actually the first letter of each word
- first and last sounds in each word, sometimes with spaces to signal words
- mixture of correctly spelt words and approximated spelling.

(Richard Parker describes the stages of spelling development in chapter 9 of this book.)

Some children, however, cannot relate the letter name to the sound it represents in a word, or even distinguish the sounds in words. Lots of auditory work needs to be done or problems with literacy may develop.

How can you help at home?
- Play games such as I spy, or use any of the numerous ideas in chapter 15.
- Enjoy reading and chanting rhymes together and making up your own variations.

PARENTS AND TEACHERS IN PARTNERSHIP

As well as the suggestions listed above, there are other things you can do to ease children's transition from home to school.

Spend some time in the classroom

If you are unsure if your child is coping in the classroom, or feel your child is not advancing fast enough, approach the teacher and ask to spend some time in school. Your presence will be appreciated — thirty new children in a kindergarten class can be quite a handful! Your involvement will let you see at first hand what is happening, how the other children are coping and where your child fits into the group.

Get to know the teacher

Your child's teacher should be a friend whom you both share. The benefits of a good relationship between teacher and parent are obvious. Don't hesitate to communicate with the teacher as you see the need — before confusion arises or problems develop.

The better the bridge between home and school, the better the education — that's the message of recent research. As teachers we will do our best to communicate with you about what we are doing in our school and why. We will try to answer your questions as completely as we can. We look forward to our partnership with you, and to your involvement in your children's education.

CHAPTER 5
The teaching of reading

Richard Parker

A while ago, my wife broke her elbow and required surgery. Having experienced surgery myself, I told her what to expect. Later, I asked her how it had been. 'It was okay', she said, 'but it wasn't anything like you said it would be'. On reflection, this was hardly surprising. My experience had been twenty-five years earlier.

Things have changed in medicine, and they have changed for the better. The same is true of the teaching of reading. What is happening in reading classrooms today is very different to what happened when we adults were at school. We now know much more about how children learn the texts they read. Informed teachers have abandoned 'round-robin reading', they have thrown away their flashcards and phonics charts and primers, and they are busy filling their classrooms with real books for children. The days of the multi-level reading scheme are numbered, and there is an air of quiet confidence that the children in today's primary classrooms will be better prepared than ever before to read the large range of materials that confronts adults in their daily lives.

SO WHAT'S NEW?

Teachers read books to children

Occasionally, when the whole class had been very 'good' (I think that actually meant she was exhausted), our teacher read to us. This usually happened at the end of the day, and with much greater frequency after the end-of-year exams.

Now, teachers read aloud to children every day. Reading aloud to children is a deliberate part of the reading program, not something tacked on to the end of the day when it's not worth starting anything else. What do children learn from this?

First of all, they discover *why* it would be worth learning to read. For some children, this realisation will come from their very first story. For others, it may come from their first experience of science fiction or fantasy, and for others, from hearing a book about a factual topic such as space travel or animals.

Children also learn what books *sound like*. The language of books is very different to the language of conversation. Young children need exposure to an enormous amount of spoken language before they begin to speak. They need considerable exposure to the sound of different types of texts before they are ready to begin reading and writing them.

In the early grades, children also learn a great deal about *how* people read from being read to, particularly when the teacher reads from a Big Book. Big Books are outsized editions of books which allow teachers to read to a group of children in the same way that parents read to their children at home. This is sometimes described as the 'shared book approach'.

Silent reading time

Many schools encourage the establishment of a silent reading time — a time when children and teachers alike select a book and read quietly until the teacher indicates that the session is over. This is sometimes called USSR *(uninterrupted, sustained silent reading)*, DEAR *(drop everything and read)* or even WEIRD *(we enjoy independent reading daily)*. Whatever the name, the ideas are the same: the teacher demonstrates that nothing interferes with reading time, children learn to select reading material carefully, and everyone relishes the opportunity of a quiet read.

How do you know that children are reading? This is a question parents often ask. The answer is simple. When children are bored, it is most uncommon for them to sit silently for an extended period of time. So if there are no disruptions, then it is almost certain that the children are reading.

Does it work? The research shows that it does, but if you are unsure, why not ask the children themselves? Most will be enthusiastic about this part of the school day.

Oral reading

Today's classrooms are characterised by a much greater emphasis on silent reading, and a corresponding decrease in emphasis on children reading orally before their peers. Of course, there are still occasions when children are invited to read aloud, and other occasions when the whole class reads aloud together. The fact is, however, that most adult reading is silent, and the research evidence indicates that it is silent reading of meaningful material which brings about improvements in reading ability. Consequently, teachers make provision for numerous opportunities during the school day for children to read silently.

Does this mean that they don't have a reading lesson? Of course not. But instead of treating reading as an isolated activity, children read in USSR, as part of a problem-solving activity in maths, as they gather information for a research project in social studies or science, and as they follow a set of instructions in craft or PE — the school day is filled with opportunities to read.

Reading conferences

Today's classrooms are likely to feature reading conferences. (Reading and writing conferences are discussed by Jan Turbill and Lorraine McDonald in chapters 7 and 10 of this book.) These conferences are based on careful observation of what individual

24

children are doing as they read. When it is appropriate, the teacher intervenes. The teacher may encourage individuals to reflect on their reading strategies. At other times, the teacher may demonstrate how to do something, or suggest an alternative strategy. In conferences, questions are far more common than directions.

Comprehension questions

The dreaded 'ten comprehension questions' are almost a thing of the past. Instead, the teacher asks the children questions *before* they read. This encourages them to use what they already know to make even greater sense of the text.

This emphasis on making sense of the text is important. The teacher is unlikely to worry about word-for-word accuracy provided that children succeed in their quest for detailed understanding. This is because teachers understand that a skilled reader does not read every word on the page; the important thing is that the reader successfully reconstructs the ideas of the author.

'Real' books

Contrived books and materials designed solely to teach reading are being replaced with 'real' texts designed for their own purposes. This includes storybooks written with the express purpose of entertaining children, and factual books designed to satisfy children's curiosity about the world in which they live.

Teachers prefer real books because they are easier for children to read, they involve children much more effectively and they are more typical of the reading material that children are likely to encounter when they become adults.

The teacher's role

The role of the teacher has changed since my schooldays. Then, teachers *directed*. They told children what to do and made sure that it was done. Many children learnt to read quite well under those conditions; but many determined never to read again once they left school.

Later there were the teachers who saw their role as that of *facilitator*. They provided children with a rich learning environment, then stood by as children explored it. Some children stumbled across reading; others simply stumbled.

What will characterise today's teachers is their capacity for effective *intervention*. This approach is based on extensive understanding of the nature of the reading process and the characteristics of written language. It is based equally on sensitive understanding and observation of children as learners, and the insight to recognise when and how children's learning needs to be supported.

These teachers will not be satisfied with the mere fact that children *can* read. They will be satisfied only if children *want* to read, and continue to do so after they leave school.

CHAPTER 6
Any problems?

Mary Anne Wilkie

It is always an exciting and joyful time both for parents and teachers when a young child begins to read. Many children learn to read incidentally and spontaneously from a very young age. This occurs with children who have:
* experimented with language in different forms (such as singing nursery rhymes, playing with sounds and words)
* learnt letter-sound patterns
* experienced books as a source of pleasure
* built up a knowledge of print
* acquired a growing knowledge of signs and labels
* learnt to recognise whole words (the names of people, animals and so on)
* become confident in the use of oral language

When these children reach school they will use all these strategies and skills automatically, without giving them specific attention. However, this is not the case for all children. Some find learning to read or write more difficult than others. There is no clear explanation for this. Children master reading and writing at different times, just as they master walking and talking at different times.

This being the case, how does a parent or a teacher recognise that a child has a 'reading problem'?

WARNING SIGNS

One of the most common indicators is when children show an unwillingness to read or to have anything to do with print. They will do anything *but* read.

Other indicators may be when children:
* exhibit poor oral reading
* have difficulty understanding what is read
* lack effective reading strategies
* lack an adequate reading vocabulary
* exhibit signs of frustration and anxiety
* recognise few words, as whole words
* constantly try to decipher any word by 'sounding it out'
* cannot tell when they have made a mistake which disturbs the meaning and make no attempt to correct themselves — they do not read for understanding

- invest much energy in the learning situation without achieving any acceptable outcome

WHAT CAUSES READING PROBLEMS?

The causes of reading problems are many and varied. They may include any of the following:
- lack of appropriate models
- high anxiety
- low motivation
- unrealistic expectations
- lack of effective prediction strategies
- inappropriate instruction and activities
- limited experience with print
- limited choice of reading materials
- lack of perseverance in a task
- learning lists of meaningless words
- limited strategies for coping with unknown words

HOW DO WE ADDRESS THESE PROBLEMS?

One of the best ways of assisting children's development is to build on what they already know and can do. Children must believe that they *can* learn. They must see themselves as successful learners — successful readers. Self-esteem is of paramount importance.

Teachers observe children to gain an insight into their development and can then support them by giving feedback about what they have already achieved. Teachers can also give support by offering strategies for solving a particular problem, by providing a model for the individual child.

Children must be confident and know that they are allowed to:
- make errors
- correct errors
- experiment with print
- pause, hesitate and use repetition

Teachers need to be sensitive observers of early behaviour and to reinforce each individual's efforts. In today's classrooms children learn at their own individual level and build on what they already know; teachers facilitate children's learning.

Help is at hand

Currently, in many schools, additional teachers offer the classroom teacher support in many varied ways, allowing small group work and individualised teaching as well as whole group sessions. Parents are also involved in day-to-day classroom learning.

In addition, many schools have a 'special needs' teacher who can help a classroom teacher devise a meaningful program for an individual child who is experiencing difficulties in learning to read or write.

Many agencies connected to schools offer support to children, teachers and parents. Specific programs around Australia include the following:

- The Three-way Reading Program, which involves the child, parents and teacher, is conducted at Special Assistance Units. Consultants work with parents and teachers over a period of time to ensure that children gain the maximum benefit from the energy they invest in the program.
- The Reading Recovery Program, aimed at Year 1, is conducted by specially trained teachers and targets children considered at risk.
- Reading without Tears is conducted at School Support Centres by teachers from the Special Education Units.

The classroom teacher may refer children to teachers at the Special Education Units and/or to educational psychologists for a full academic assessment. Following the assessment an individual program can be devised and implemented.

Most schools offer information sessions throughout the year. Conducted by classroom teachers, subject coordinators and/or specialists from some of the support agencies mentioned above, these sessions cover a wide variety of subject areas.

HOW CAN PARENTS HELP?

It is important that a parent (or preferably, both parents) attend these sessions. Approach them with a positive attitude. Questions will probably occur to you, often some time after the information session. Don't be afraid to raise those questions. Make an appointment to speak to the teacher at a later date. Ask for some further literature or references to inform yourself better or to clarify a point of concern or interest.

If you are concerned that your child has a problem in any area of the curriculum, contact the class teacher as soon as possible. Organise to meet at a mutually convenient time, and approach the situation calmly and pleasantly. It is a good idea to jot down areas of concern before the meeting and take your list with you to ensure that all your concerns are considered.

Allow the teacher sufficient time to organise additional support if that is deemed necessary. Approach the meeting with an open mind.

Keep the lines open

Maintain contact with your child's teacher. Good lines of communication between parents and teacher will give the child a better chance of overcoming any learning problems than contact which is sporadic or negative.

Learning improves when parents and teachers communicate and collaborate effectively, integrating the home and the school environment.

CHAPTER 7
The teaching of writing: Process writing explained

Jan Turbill

WHAT IS PROCESS WRITING?

'Process writing' is a phrase you may already recognise if you have been following educational trends over the last few years. It describes an approach to the teaching of writing in schools.

The basis of the approach is simple: writing is a process in which meaning is constructed with words for others to read. It involves us in rehearsing, drafting, revising, editing, proofreading and sharing.

When proficient adult writers write, they go through various steps or actions; they go through a *process*. They always have a reason to write and they always have an audience. For example I may wish to write:

- a card to Aunt Lucy; for Aunt Lucy to read
- a shopping list; for myself
- a letter of complaint to the Council; for the Shire Clerk and Councillors

WHAT DOES IT INVOLVE?

We begin by *rehearsing* our writing: we think about what we want to say, what we need to write. We often talk about the topic with others before starting. We may also read for further information. We may need to research our topic: check relevant facts; check whether there is any Vegemite left; find out the Shire Clerk's name.

Next we begin to put words down. We don't usually worry about neat handwriting and correct spelling at this stage. We are writing a *draft* and we concentrate on getting our message down so that it says what we intend it to say. If we are unsure of a word we usually just have a go at it; we *invent* it for the moment. There will be time later to work on the writing — to change the words around, to add information, to check spelling and punctuation.

Correct spelling, punctuation and clear handwriting are necessary for writing, but the emphasis on correctness and neatness varies according to the purpose of the writing and the stage we have reached in that piece of writing. We may choose to leave the writing in its draft stage — I don't do any more to my shopping list because I know I need 'lasana' and 'potatoes', whether the spelling is correct or not. But I will work on my draft letter of complaint to the Council because I want to be sure that the intended message is clear. So I *revise* and *edit* my writing: I read it and reread it; I change words, move sentences around, add more information in one paragraph and delete words from another. I might read it to a trusted peer and ask whether the message is clear.

Satisfied now with my letter, which has been through several drafts, I finally write it out in clear legible handwriting and conventional spelling on a sheet of white unlined paper. Before I sign my name on the letter and put it in the envelope, I will carefully *proofread* it to check that all the surface features (spelling and punctuation) are correct. My letter is ready to 'go public' — to be read by the intended audience. I have *published* it and I wait for a response to my writing.

At all times in this process I am responsible for my writing — for what I say and how I set it out. I make the decision to change things, to leave them or, if necessary, to tear up the draft and start again.

The writing has succeeded in its purpose when it has been read and understood by the intended audience: I've used my shopping list; the council responds to my request.

WHAT DOES ALL THIS MEAN FOR THE TEACHING OF WRITING IN OUR SCHOOLS?

We want children:
- to write as writers in the real world do — to rehearse, draft, revise, edit, proofread and share
- to practise writing daily for a variety of purposes and a wide range of audiences
- to take responsibility for, and control of, their own writing
- to have the opportunity to choose their own topics
- to 'have a go' at new ideas, at new types of writing (poems, letters, reports, narratives) and new spellings
- to discuss their drafts with their peers and their teacher in a *conference*

What is the conference?

The conference is a teaching-talking time between the teacher and a child, the teacher and a group of children or between children. During this time children share and discuss their ideas about what they want to write, what they have written, or how they can improve their writing. Constructive criticism is given by the teacher to the novice writer. Questions asked might include: 'What did you mean when you said . . .?' 'Why did you say . . .?' 'Who is . . .?'

The older child is expected to change information, add information and generally work on the writing in order to make sure the message is clear. The younger writer in the conference time will simply share the piece of writing. ('What did you write about? Would you read it to me, please? Tell me about your drawing.') The teacher might also comment on some of the child's attempted spellings. ('That's a good try at spelling *Christmas*. I'll show you how I write it.')

The conference is a teaching time in which the teacher works with children at their individual level and pace. (Lorraine McDonald gives a more detailed description of conferencing in chapter 10 of this book.)

WHAT ABOUT QUALITY?

With process writing teachers are aiming to improve the quality of children's writing. Children spend more time writing than ever before, and more time working on a piece of writing, so that the quality of that piece is the best the children can achieve at that stage of their development. Our aim is to develop independent writers — children who enjoy writing and can see a purpose for doing it.

Process writing has also been called 'conference writing' and 'story writing'. Whatever the name, the philosophy behind the approach is simply that writing is a process and that children need the opportunity to experience that process so that they can take responsibility for shaping their writing into products which satisfy them as writers.

CHAPTER 8
What's all this 'genre' stuff?

Ross Weightman

WHAT DOES 'GENRE' MEAN?

Apart from hearing it used occasionally by film or literary critics, most of us would have heard little of the word *genre*. If you keep an ear open at your local school, however, you may know that genre has been a bit of a buzz word in literacy in recent years. You may even know that the term can quickly stimulate debate among certain teachers. But what you may not know is what all this genre stuff means.

Genre simply means 'family group' or 'kind'. In the area of education it refers to kinds of writing. The important genres are:
- *narratives* — any of the wide range of stories
- *reports* — including definitions and descriptions
- *procedures* — instructions and directions
- *expositions* — these argue a point of view
- *discussions* — these weigh up different points of view
- *explanations* — these give reasons for things

While that is a brief description of what genres are, their importance lies not in their fancy name, but in the package of ideas known as the *genre-based approach to teaching writing*. This package is tied together by the strong threads of linguistic theory and educational philosophy. That may sound very heavy, but it is important to understand something of the ideas which have helped develop this approach.

WHY IS GENRE IMPORTANT?

Those who advocate the genre-based approach believe strongly that being able to use language — especially in its written form — will open doors for people to succeed in the workforce and beyond. In fact, the teaching of genres is strongly associated with the idea of social power.

The argument is essentially this: if individuals can learn to control particular genres that society sees as important, then their chances of success in society are greatly improved. It is obvious, for example, that the person who can write an effective job application has a good chance of getting the job.

WHAT ABOUT PROCESS WRITING?

When the genre approach was first introduced into primary schools, some educators portrayed 'genre' and 'process' as opposing and contradictory philosophies. Since that time, many teachers throughout Australia have proved them wrong. Both approaches can be combined to provide children with a balanced, effective and stimulating writing program. (In chapter 10, Lorraine McDonald shows how the two approaches meet.)

WHAT HAPPENS IN THE CLASSROOM?

In the classroom, the genre-based approach involves a lot more than just getting students to change the form of their writing. The procedure that teachers follow actually involves three important phases of the learning experience. These are:
- the modelling phase
- the joint-writing phase
- the independent writing phase

The modelling phase

With the teaching of genre, teachers are very concerned with the groundwork they lay and the preparation they give their students. When young children learn to talk, their utterances are a response to particular situations or contexts. Genre teachers believe that context is just as important when learning to write. Consequently, the context for a particular genre must be set by manipulating classroom learning experiences to make sure that children are aware of a number of things. These are:
- the purpose of a particular genre
- the form that particular genre takes
- the grammatical pattern peculiar to that genre

Activities will involve listening to, reading, discussing and interacting with examples of a particular genre. When teaching the 'procedure' genre, for instance, recipes or car instruction manuals may be studied. These may be presented on the board, as an overhead transparency or in some other way which enables ideas to be shared.

The joint-writing phase

In this phase, the teacher and children write a text together. Again, the board or an overhead transparency is used as the teacher guides and helps to organise ideas supplied by the children. This may involve questioning, rewording, summarising, prompting and acting as a consultant. From this, the children gain the confidence and knowledge to help them write independently.

The independent writing phase

Here children are given the chance to write individually. While they may have a choice of topic, the writing must be in the same genre as the jointly written text. This phase involves gathering information, drafting and revising writing and consulting with the teacher or peers when necessary.

When finished, the work will be 'published'. The form of publishing will vary according to the genre chosen. For instance, a unit on narratives might result in a class anthology, while a unit on expositions might result in a number of letters to the editor of the local newspaper arguing for more play equipment in the local park.

Through this three-stage process, children increasingly gain control over a genre as they develop their knowledge of its purpose, form and grammar and learn how to organise and present that knowledge in written form.

WHAT DID YOU SAY ABOUT GRAMMAR?

Grammar has been mentioned a number of times in this chapter and it needs to be explained. Grammar is seen as being important for both teachers and children. Teachers, it is argued, need to know precisely how to teach and evaluate writing. Knowledge of grammar plays an important part in this. Children, when writing, need to know how to construct meaning in an appropriate way. Knowledge of grammar extends their range of options when doing this.

It is in the area of grammar that genre teachers often come in for some criticism, because many people see this approach as a return to the days of parsing and analysis. This is not the case. The type of grammar that genre teachers consider most useful in assisting young writers is not traditional 'school grammar', but *systemic-functional grammar*.

The big name aside, this is an alternative form of grammar developed by noted linguists. It is not about brainstorming better words for *said,* for example, but rather about understanding how elements of a piece of writing interrelate in order to produce an effective whole. Unlike traditional grammar, systemic-functional grammar is not taught as a separate subject, but as an aspect of the writing that children are working on. They learn how language patterns vary from genre to genre and how certain language elements are more useful than others when writing for a particular audience.

Many teachers and parents fear that learning grammar will enslave young children to a new discipline involving hard-to-pronounce terms, abstract concepts and boring schoolwork. Again, this is not the case. As young writers in the infants and junior primary grades become familiar with common genres through their writing, their attention is drawn to aspects of grammar in an informal way. As their awareness grows, children learn more sophisticated concepts which require grammatical terms as labels. In this way, children's control over the accepted, standard forms of grammar in language evolves from their practical experience of writing in different genres.

In a society where writing is highly valued, the genre-based approach offers today's children the chance not only to be well equipped to cope with different writing demands, but also to succeed in their individual endeavours in tomorrow's world.

CHAPTER 9
The teaching of spelling

Richard Parker

Miss P was my Grade 3 teacher back in 1950. I remember a number of things about that year. I remember how the pages of my composition book were removed, one by one, as part of Miss P's crusade to make me a tidy writer.

Another thing I recall vividly was a spelling lesson. 'Today', said Miss P, 'you will learn three words which are very easy to confuse'. She proceeded to write them on the blackboard:

guard
gauge
gaurantee — whoops! — *guarantee*.

She was half-right…I didn't learn to spell the three words, but I have remained permanently convinced that they are readily confused.

HOW DO THEY TEACH SPELLING TODAY?

You are most unlikely to see this type of teaching in today's classrooms. The teaching of spelling, both in its concepts and its practice, has changed dramatically since the time when all the Grade 3 children across a school system were certain to be attempting to memorise the same list of words. Here are some of those concepts, with their practical implications.

Individual differences

The move in the 1960s to greater individualisation of learning was a significant factor. No two children are alike. Children differ in the *way* they learn, and they differ in the *rate* at which they learn. This recognition has caused many teachers to abandon class spelling lists and the associated spelling tests that typically dominated every Friday morning.

Individual and class needs

Another influence on spelling teaching has been the general recognition that language is acquired most effectively *when it is needed*. Many teachers and parents observed that children who mastered a spelling list one week seemed to have little recall of some of the words a few weeks later. There are undoubtedly many reasons for this, but it seems likely that the major reason was that children memorised the words in the list because they had to, and not because they needed to be able to spell the words in order to do something which was important to them at that time.

Some teachers have responded to this understanding by developing spelling lists consisting of words the children are encountering in the class program. If the class is studying the creatures of the sea, then the spelling list is likely to contain words such as *whale, crustacean, dorsal* and so on. This is certainly an improvement on learning words which bear no relationship to anything else that is happening in the classroom.

Other teachers reject the notion of having the whole class memorise the same list, and instead build up *words banks*. These are based on unusual words encountered in classroom texts and also on children's spelling needs, which are usually expressed as, 'Please Miss, how do I spell...?' Word banks are usually displayed on the wall so that children can refer to them as the need arises.

Other teachers place great emphasis on having each child create and maintain a *personal dictionary*. These are simply exercise books, alphabetically indexed. Children are expected to add to their dictionaries whenever they encounter unfamiliar words or whenever they require assistance with spelling. They are also encouraged to check the spelling of words as they engage in writing activities. A willingness to look up words and a familiarity with alphabetical order are useful by-products of this strategy.

Spelling is learnt by attempting to spell

Perhaps the most significant influence on teaching methods in recent years has been the recognition that children learn accurate, conventional spelling by making repeated — and progressively better — attempts at spelling. As a result, informed teachers are quite happy for young children to use what some researchers have called 'invented' or 'temporary' spellings. Teachers are more likely to respond to such unconventional spellings by writing the conventional form above the child's attempt, rather than crossing out the attempt and requiring the child to rewrite the conventional form of the word a specified number of times.

Another practice, now adopted in many schools, sees each child using a 'have-a-go book'. Before any help with the spelling of a word is given, the child must first make an attempt. These attempts allow the types of teacher intervention outlined below.

THE STAGES OF SPELLING DEVELOPMENT

Recent research on spelling has revealed that there are different types of unconventional spellings, some of which are observed in the writing of inexperienced spellers and others in the work of spellers who are developing far more confidence in their spelling.

Scribble

The first stage of writing we could loosely call 'pretend' writing. This is different from a child's earliest scribble, which usually has a circular appearance. It is when a parent's inquiry, 'What have you got there?' results in the response, 'It's my story!', that we can look upon the scribble as an early form of writing. Of course, the spelling is totally unconventional — in fact, unrecognisable — and unrepeatable.

Before long the scribble becomes more horizontal, resembling wiggly lines of print. Isolated letters or figures may occur. The child's understanding of how writing works has obviously become much more sophisticated. At this stage, the child may be able to tell you what the text actually says; in some cases, the text may be reread on a subsequent occasion.

Stage 1 — deviant

In the initial stage of spelling development, letters and figures are clustered together to represent words. However, there is no relationship between the letters used and the sounds of the words. Although the spelling appears to be rather chaotic, the child demonstrates an understanding that scribble, shapes, and blobs of colour are not used in writing. Examples of children's deviant spelling include:

aml   (monster)
em3321   (united)

Stage 2 — pre-phonetic

In this stage, children demonstrate an understanding that there is some consistency between the sounds that make up spoken words and the letters that are used to write words. Typically, children get the first sound of the word appropriately represented, and perhaps the last, but never all of the sounds. Examples of pre-phonetic spelling include:

mtr   (monster)
sps   (stamps)

Teachers will respond to a spelling of this type by saying, 'That's a good try. Now listen to the word very carefully. Can you hear a sound that you don't have in your word?' This kind of response encourages children to continue with the spelling attempts while steering them in the direction of the next stage.

Stage 3 — phonetic

Once children have progressed from the random representation of the first stage to the more consistent and recognisable form of the pre-phonetic stage, the next stage usually involves spelling a particular word in such a way that *all* the sounds of the spoken word are appropriately represented in the written form. This permits children to spell approximately half their vocabulary in a conventional manner. Examples of phonetic, but unconventional, spellings include:

monstr   (monster)
lam   (lamb)

Teacher intervention at this stage focuses on the existence and identity of irregular features of the word. Teachers may respond to *monstr* by saying, 'That's a very good attempt. But you've left out a letter. Where do you think it might be?' (Child points to the space between *t* and *r.*) 'Great! What do you think the letter might be?'

Stage 4 — transitional

Many children fail to move much beyond the phonetic stage in their spelling. A look at the spelling of teenage and adult writers will reveal that most 'errors' are phonetically consistent with the pronunciation of the word.

With encouragement of the type outlined above, children will produce spellings which acknowledge that there is something unpredictable about many words. For example:

monstor   (monster)
lamd   (lamb)

Informed teachers are quick to·realise that *lamd* is a much more advanced spelling of *lamb* than *lam* because the child has already internalised the presence of a silent letter at the end of the word. It is usually not long before the transitional spelling is replaced by the final stage of conventional spelling.

It should be noted that children will exhibit different spelling stages at any one time. We might expect a Grade 3 child to have a reasonable number of conventional spellings, as well as some which are phonetic-transitional. This would also be true of adults, though we might reasonably expect a higher percentage of conventional spellings in this case.

Poor Miss P — she must be spinning in her grave!

CHAPTER 10
Parents in the classroom

Lorraine McDonald

'What did you do at school today?'
'Nothing much.'

When my children were in primary school, this was our typical daily dialogue. But when the school invited parents to help in the classroom, my sons' teachers showed me just how much work is done. I discovered also that the teaching of reading and writing has changed drastically since my primary schooldays.

WHAT'S NEW IN READING AND WRITING?

Reading in schools is very different today, both in the way children are taught and in the kinds of books they read. As Richard Parker explains in chapter 5 of this book, teachers are introducing *real* books into their classrooms and stressing the importance of *making meaning* from the printed words on the page.

Teaching of writing has also seen dramatic changes. The first change you will notice is that the term *writing* encompasses what used to be called 'written expression' or 'creative writing' or even 'composition'.

Second, there is a writing time — usually four or five times weekly — during which children may select their own topics and write drafts. These drafts are 'conferenced' and then often 'published'. (Jan Turbill describes this approach, known as 'process writing', in chapter 7 of this book.)

Third, as well as this free-choice writing there may be 'directed writing' where children are asked to write in a specific genre. (Ross Weightman explains genre in chapter 8.)

Finally, you will notice that the children are all at different stages in their writing.

HOW CAN YOU HELP WITH READING IN THE CLASSROOM?

When you are asked to help with reading, you may be asked to work with a small group or with individual children. In either case, you need to do more than merely ask children to read. You may also be asked to participate in the reading-aloud aspect of the teacher's program. Although much more emphasis is now placed on silent reading, there are skills to reading aloud which teachers may want children to practise.

39

How do you take a group for reading?

Of course, the teacher is the professional in the classroom and his or her instructions are of primary importance. It is confusing for children if different sets of demands are made of them.

However, teachers are busy people and may not be able to give you as full a briefing as you would like. As well, teachers are very comfortable talking with children, but often less so when interacting with adults. They may not want to insult your intelligence by giving too much detail about what is obvious to them.

The following ideas about reading are offered to back up the teacher's directions and to supplement any information you are given.

Before reading: discussion and prediction

The first step is to talk about the text. Whether children each have a different book or whether they have multiple copies of the same one, you can ask them to look at any pictures, read the title and think about what the text may be about. Together you can predict what the page or story will say. If the children have read their books previously, then ask them to tell you any details or events they can remember.

This pre-reading discussion, which should only take a few minutes, is crucial. It prepares children to read by using their existing knowledge as a background to reading a text. Current research indicates that this is a vital support for successful reading.

Reading silently

The second step is to ask each child to read the text silently. 'Read it in your mind' is one way of putting it. This allows them to concentrate on the meaning of the print, rather than on pronouncing the words. If you have been directed to ask the children to read aloud, then they can do so *after* reading silently (reading aloud is discussed in detail below). If a child has a problem with a word, ask him or her to look ahead silently, then return to the problem word and think of a word *which makes sense* in the context. You may need to give some clues by referring to a picture or hinting about the context, for example:

'What sounds do dogs make?'
'Does that word begin with *b?*'
'So what makes sense?'
'Yes, *bark* — good, you worked it out!'

Notice how you focus on the meaning of the text first, then draw attention to the initial letter to confirm the prediction. These days we don't ask children to sound out words in reading, but to think of what best fits the sense of what they are reading and to combine this with their knowledge of print.

Checking understanding

The next step is to focus on comprehension. To check children's understanding you can ask them to retell the text to you. Retelling is a good strategy because you can ask for the main ideas or probe for details, depending on your purpose. It is easy to hear how well children have comprehended the text, and sharing the retelling can support those who have missed an aspect of the story.

You can also lead a discussion which brings in the children's own responses to the text, using such questions as 'I wonder why that happened?' or 'Does this character remind you of anyone you know?' These sorts of questions do not have a correct answer, but encourage children to reflect on what they have read and relate it to their own lives. In this way even very young children can respond thoughtfully.

Reading aloud

Teachers may also ask you to take a group for reading aloud. The pre-reading discussion, silent reading and comprehension check are still essential components of the oral reading program.

If the group is reading from multiple copies of the same book, you may like to make the oral reading interesting for them by giving them different parts to read — one or two may read the narration, while others read the dialogue — thus turning the reading into a mini-play. With this technique children do as much reading as they do when taking turns ('round-robin reading'), but have a lot more fun doing so.

Whether working with a group or an individual child, your participation as one of the readers will provide a model of expressive reading.

Finally, even competent readers find word-for-word accuracy hard when reading aloud. Silent practice gives them a chance to attain accuracy. As well, we listen for approximations of words which make sense. For example when *Dad* is substituted for *Father* we know the child is understanding the meaning on the page. After the reading is completed, then it is appropriate to return to some misread words and look at them in turns of 'correctness'.

Other reading activities

You may be asked to read aloud to a group of children and to talk about the story afterwards. To do this well you need to read the story to yourself at least once for fluency and expression. When discussing the text, use the questions suggested above in 'Checking understanding'.

You may also be asked to supervise a group or individuals completing different reading activities set up by the teacher.

Alternatively, children may be responding in writing to a text they have read. Again, the initial emphasis is on the meaning of what is said, before the writing is edited and presented in a final draft.

HOW CAN YOU HELP WITH WRITING IN THE CLASSROOM?

When you are asked to help with writing in the classroom you will often be asked to help in the interaction known as 'conferencing'. Conferencing involves talking with children about their written piece and helping them extend, improve or shape their writing. You may be asked to work with an individual child or with a group, where you lead four or five children in a discussion about their writing. The group conference may be called a 'writers' circle'.

Teachers will often suggest questions that they want you to ask and it is a good idea to request some guidance here. This shows that you acknowledge their expertise and leadership in the classroom and that you want to fit in with their teaching style. As with reading, the following ideas are intended to supplement the teacher's directions.

What does a conference involve?

There are three aspects to conferencing. The first — and the most important, as it helps children work on the ideas in their writing — is that conference questions focus on the *meaning* of what has been written. The second aspect concerns the *style* of the writing — the choice of words, the variety of vocabulary, the appropriateness of the form to the content. The third aspect concentrates on *editing* the writing — spelling, punctuation, speech marks and paragraphing are the concerns here as the piece is prepared for publication.

Sometimes the teacher may ask you to focus on one of these aspects only; more often, however, meaning and style are combined in the one conference.

How do you begin to lead a conference?

The conference usually begins with a child reading aloud his or her piece of writing. This is a good starting technique as it allows each child to 'hear' the text. Children often correct themselves during this reading — you hear them mutter, 'That doesn't make sense' and see them bend over the page to adjust what they have written. As the reading proceeds, you listen carefully according to the purpose of your conference. Sometimes you will need to listen for different purposes with different children, depending on the stage of their writing.

Focus on meaning

As a general rule, you listen for the *meaning* of the text and notice any obvious gaps in the sense of the piece. If it is a story, for example, you listen for a logical plot sequence; characters who connect in some way; a satisfactory resolution. If it is another type or genre of writing (say, instructions on how to play a game), then you listen for an ordered sequence and appropriate language and terminology.

Basic principles for listening are 'Does it make sense?' and 'Is anything missing here?'. Teachers often jot down a point that they want to raise later, and you might like to do this too.

Once the piece is read, the conference begins. When listening, remember two things: *be positive, be precise.*

1   Your first comment is a positive one:
    'I like your beginning — I could picture that spaceship.'
    'What a lot of action you have in this story — I really like that.'
    'I like your dialogue — I felt I was listening to the conversation.'

'What good words you used to describe how the computer game is played — *fast and furious* — well done!'

Always listen for something positive to say and be precise in your praise. If you are with a group you could ask them what they enjoyed about the piece that was read. Initially, children will offer general comments like 'I thought it was good' or 'I liked it', but gradually they will start to copy your precise comments and will soon come up with original and pertinent ideas of their own.

2 The next step is to ask a question about one aspect of the piece of writing. This is usually a question about the meaning of the piece, for example:

'Where did Jones come from? I didn't notice how he was connected to the story.'

'Is there anything else you could tell the reader about computer games?'

'I didn't understand this part. What were you trying to say here?'

If working with a group, encourage them to ask questions of each other as writers. Children often 'get stuck' and can neither answer your question nor think of any further ideas. You can offer some ideas or ask the group to suggest possibilities:

'How could Faisal bring Jones into the story earlier so we know who he is?'

'Who can think of something else Lisa can write about computer games?'

'How could Tim make this clearer? What could he write?'

When conferencing, I encourage the writer to make a note on the page about the suggestions so that they won't be forgotten.

3 Finally, if it is a group conference the next writer reads and the process repeats itself until all have had a turn. It usually takes up to thirty minutes to conference four or five children.

Sometimes you will not have a question to ask, yet your instincts will tell you that the piece needs more work. One technique to help writers is to ask them what they like about their own text. Usually primary children can tell you the 'best' part of their own writing and that gives you an opening to suggest how to make the whole piece more exciting or interesting by extending that section.

Focus on style

You will often notice the *style* of a piece of writing when it needs 'fixing'. When children are composing they concentrate on the meaning of what they are saying. Combining meaning with style — careful choice of words and variety of expression — only comes with practice, maturity and advice. When the content of the piece is satisfactory given the writer's age, ability and stage of development (the teacher can advise you here), you may choose to conference the writer on the language of the writing.

One of children's common stylistic patterns is to begin many sentences in the same way. In a conference you can comment on how often they begin a sentence with *I* or *They,* for example, and ask for suggestions for rephrasing the sentences, for example:

- Text: 'I was walking in the forest. I saw the robot coming after me.'
- Suggestion: 'Walking in the forest, I saw the robot coming after me.'

Once children see how to rephrase two or three sentence beginnings they can usually change many of the others themselves.

Another common tendency is to use the same expression or words repeatedly and close together, which creates a boring effect. A brainstorming session for similar words can show the writer how to vary the vocabulary. For instance, *forest* in the example above could become *woods, bush, trees* or *scrub* — all of which have variations in meaning but could be appropriate, depending on the text. This is a suitable time to show your writers how to use a thesaurus — a useful skill, best taught in context.

Focus on genre

Writing conferences usually concentrate on meaning and style. If teachers wish you to conference on a particular *genre,* as well as the ideas above you should expect to be given some more specific suggestions which relate directly to the genre being written. These suggestions will guide you as to how children's writing is to be organised and any special features of language they are expected to incorporate.

Focus on editing

During the term, each child will be asked to 'publish' one or more pieces of writing. This means that each child will be required to spend some time working on the spelling, punctuation, paragraphing and presentation of the piece. Requirements will differ, depending on the children's writing experience, age and stage of development. Teachers will usually give clear directions as to the help you can give in this area. They may want you to work with individuals in the layout and design of a book; you may be asked to type out children's texts as a final copy; you could be a support for a child carefully rewriting a final draft.

The *editing* conference highlights the place and importance of the traditional presentation skills of written language. The main purpose of an editing conference is to help the children *proofread* their work. Again, teachers will guide you as to how 'perfect' the final copy will be. Naturally, expectations may differ from class to class and child to child, as teachers allow for individual differences. On the other hand, teachers may set a standard for everyone to attain, depending on their knowledge of the children.

The two main areas to be covered in an editing conference are spelling and punctuation.

1   Spelling. This is an area which creates much anxiety for parents, teachers and children alike. As Jan Turbill notes (chapter 7), children are now encouraged to attempt spellings of words as they write, rather than restrict themselves to the words they can spell. They do this by phonetically spelling the words they want to use, in the first instance, then applying spelling patterns and knowledge of English words as they gain more experience in reading and writing.

The editing conference is the right time to concentrate on spelling. You can ask individuals to proofread their piece and to mark the words they think need correction. Depending on the level of the class and the individuals, the teacher may wish you to help a child standardise these words only. With a different child, the teacher may ask you to help correct all the misspelt words. In either case, write the standard spelling on a piece of paper for the child to copy, rather than say the letters. This helps to imprint the word visually in the memory.

Again, teachers' routines are paramount here — they will have developed class strategies and will know individual children's capabilities.

2 Punctuation. You can help children punctuate by having them listen to themselves (or you) read their piece aloud, pausing at appropriate places and inserting the commas, quotation marks and full stops where necessary. Depending on the level of the class, it may also be appropriate to suggest paragraph breaks.

Are beginning writers different?

Conferencing beginning writers (or those who have less well-developed literacy skills in English than their peers) is essentially the same as conferencing older or mainstream children. The initial focus is always on the meaning of the piece, though young children are not expected to rewrite or redraft their work.

Teachers often ask parents to write a standard version of what the child tells you the marks on the page mean. Another interesting technique is to write a dialogue: that is, a relevant question or comment incorporating the language of the piece. The child is encouraged to respond further and this becomes the extended draft of the written text. For example:

Evett (age 5): 'Little Red Riding Hood was having a birthday party.'
Teacher: 'Who was at Little Red Riding Hood's birthday party?'
Evett: 'Grandma.'

Conferencing is not difficult, but it is time-consuming. Your participation is valuable because it can give children increased contact with a mature language user and the opportunity to hear another point of view about their writing.

IN CONCLUSION

Parents *can* contribute in the classroom — to the teacher, their own children and their children's peers.

An extra hand can help the teacher in a variety of ways — from the 'busy' task of constructing a book from a child's writing, to discussing a book with a group of children. Your help frees teachers to work more closely with children who need some extra attention.

As well, your own children receive the message that their education is important to you and they see a connection between home and school which may reduce any conflict between the two spheres.

Teachers know that parents are already effective educators of their children. They are aware of their own professional responsibility in the classroom and they have devoted some years to gaining the expertise to fulfil it. Parents can acknowledge this by giving their support and cooperation when they become 'classroom helpers'.

CHAPTER 11
School reports

Mandy Tunica

'A school report should strengthen the cooperative bond existing between school and home in relation to the education of a particular child.' (E. Tomlinson, 'Learning: A Child's Progress', Leader, 3:35-7, 1966.)

As a parent you are entitled to feedback on your child's progress at *any time* during the year. To understand how well your child is developing, you will need to know the educational objectives of the school and the requirements of particular subjects. If you are confused, curious or concerned about what your child is learning, the homework set, or the methods of assessing achievement on any aspect of the school's educational program, contact the principal and ask for an explanation or clarification of the programs, policies and teaching strategies.

CHILDREN WITH SPECIAL NEEDS

Perhaps you feel that your child needs additional assistance in a specific area. Most schools have highly skilled support teachers to help students whose first language is not English, to provide extra advice on the teaching of Aboriginal students and to work closely with those students who have learning difficulties. Ask the principal whether such specialist teachers are available and if so, whether your child has access to their services.

If there are problems at home or school which you feel might affect your child's behaviour, attitude or learning, arrange for an interview with the school counsellor, who will advise you and alert the staff to potential problems.

WHAT TO EXPECT FROM SCHOOL REPORTS

Reports vary from school to school. There is the continuous, personal, informal report and the more traditional, formal kind, usually issued twice a year. Some schools issue descriptive reports; others encourage self-evaluation by students; and many schools today encourage three-way reports where teachers, students and parents all have their say.

Informal reports

Informal, continuous reporting might include telephone calls, letters from the school or a conference or interview with a particular teacher before or after school. Teachers' comments on your children's written work should give you an ongoing indication of obvious strengths and weaknesses and ways in which they can improve. Many schools also give weekly awards or certificates for achievement and performance.

Formal reports

The formal school report generally gives numerical marks or grades which reflect children's academic performance, often in relation to others in the class or grade. Written comments should accompany each mark so that both children and parents clearly understand the reasons for the 'results'. After all, a number in isolation has no meaning. Advice should be offered as to *how* parents can assist. Comments like 'can do better', 'makes little effort', 'untidy', 'careless' are basically negative and offer no guidance for parents. If children are to improve, they need encouragement, the preservation of their self-esteem, reasons for any problems, and suggestions on how they can be helped and by whom. In this way the report becomes a meaningful part of a continuing exchange between teacher, parent and child. Studies on the value of school reports show that children improve most noticeably when there is a high degree of communication and cooperation.

The formal report may also include comments on children's attitude, conduct and attendance as well as a general comment on their social and physical development. Space is left for parental comment, and notification made of arrangements to discuss the reports with teachers — usually at a parent-teacher meeting.

Descriptive reports

Some schools issue a descriptive report where, as well as or instead of marks, the teacher writes a profile of the student in terms of the skills being developed in certain subject areas. These reports tend to stress strengths rather than weaknesses, reflect *individual* development and emphasise children's progress towards realising their own potential rather than ranking or comparing their capabilities against the peer group. It is more useful to have this information on what your children *can* do, rather than be told that they came fifteenth out of thirty in the class and that they are 'average' or 'satisfactory'.

Another advantage of the descriptive report is that it often gives insights into areas that cannot be tested and so points more clearly to matters needing improvement.

Self-evaluation

Many schools now actively involve students in self-evaluation, taking their immediate consumers into partnership in the learning process. Once the objectives of the subject are explained to them, even young students are well equipped to write reports on themselves. Reading, writing, speaking and listening are the basic skills involved in language development or the subject English K-12. Aware of these skills and the course requirements, this student reflects on her progress and achievement:

I'm pleased with my development this year. I think I have improved in my writing. I really don't have much trouble with my spelling and punctuation. I read more at home and regularly borrow books from the library. I read the paper and borrow books from my cousins who've got a whole stack of books. I don't really participate in discussions with the whole class but I do contribute in small groups and I'm pretty good at listening. I'm reasonably well organised. I hand in my book on time and always bring pen and books to school. Sometimes I should concentrate more and try to join in class discussions. Also I should think more before writing.

Three-way reports

Some schools involve parents more actively in the reporting process. They provide guidelines to assist parents in observing their children's learning at home and invite them to comment on their progress. These comments are then shared with children and teachers in a three-way conference. In this way everyone who has a stake in the child's development is able to share in its evaluation.

EXAMPLES OF REPORTS FROM PRIMARY SCHOOLS

The report issued by Coogee South Public School (NSW) begins with a general comment to parents reminding them that 'all learning occurs at an individual rate, through recognisable stages of development and achievement' and includes teacher comments on the six broad learning areas as well as on personal and social development. Space is provided for the student ('My own report'), the principal and the parent.

Daceyville Public School (NSW) has an introduction explaining the place of the report in the education of the child:

This report supplements other forms of communication concerning your child's progress at school. As each person develops in different ways at different rates, we ask that you do not compare his/her report with those of other children, but consider the progress of your child as an individual.

Modern teaching theory considers that children learn more effectively through active inquiry in small groups. Thus each student's performance is assessed within his/her particular group in each subject area.

Assessments have been made in two strands of the curriculum:

1   Academic including communicating, investigating and expressing.
2   Social including work and study habits, and social attitudes and behaviour.

Both strands are of equal importance in the total development of your child.

The child's self-assessment space includes sentence beginnings which the child completes. For example:

'I'm good at ...'
'I'm terrific at ...'
'I like ...'
'I could be better at ...'

The values taught at the school are included in a checklist and there is ample room for teachers' and parents' comments.

A model for school reports

With the support of the Disadvantaged Schools Program, the staff of Glebe Public School (NSW) prepared a school report which is so comprehensive, informative and constructive that in 1988 it won an award from the Director-General of the New South Wales Department of School Education. A long process of consultation with parents, inservicing of staff and trialling of different forms led to the final product.

The report is a booklet, put together by children and teachers, which goes home once a term in infants and half-yearly in the primary grades. One page in the infants report contains 'messages from' the support teachers (for example teachers of English as a second language), the class teacher, the principal and the students; whereas the primary report includes comparative grading and basic skills.

The names, photographs and roles of the specialist teachers are included, as is information about the school's teaching strategies (such as process writing) and procedures (such as the code of discipline). The parents' page asks questions and seeks advice about continuing evaluation of the report format. Photographs of children in various group activities, copies of merit certificates and a letter from the class teacher complete the booklet. The report is translated into various languages to meet the needs of the school's inner-city community.

HAVE YOUR SAY

If you are unhappy with the type of report being issued by your school, why not raise the issue with the principal, the parents' body or the school council? You may find you are voicing the concerns of many — staff and parents — and the outcome might well be a more useful format. Schools can change their methods of reporting.

Finally, do not be depressed by what appears to be a dismal report; do not despair of your child's future. Many successful and famous people received poor reports at school. The books of the late Roald Dahl are loved by young and old. Here are some extracts from his end-of-term reports for 'English composition' — just to show that teachers can sometimes be wrong!

'I have never met a boy who so persistently writes the exact opposite of what he means. He seems incapable of marshalling his thoughts on paper.'...'A persistent muddler. Vocabulary negligible, sentences malconstructed. He reminds me of a camel.'...'This boy is an indolent and illiterate member of the class.'...'Consistently idle. Ideas limited.' (From 'Lucky Break: How I Became a Writer', in *The Wonderful Story of Henry Sugar and Six More*, Jonathan Cape, 1977.)

As Dahl himself concluded: 'Little wonder that it never entered my head to become a writer in those days'.

Acknowledgments

Thanks to Coogee South, Daceyville and Glebe Public Schools for information about their reports.

PART THREE

AT HOME
Supporting literacy

CHAPTER 12

Reading at home

Vivienne Nicoll

SUPPORTING DEVELOPING READERS

Learning to read is one of the most significant achievements of children's primary schooling. Some will find it an easy accomplishment. Others, for a combination of reasons, may find the process more daunting; they will need more support and encouragement.

We know that effective readers have two major characteristics:
● They realise that it is more important to make sense of what they read than to read precisely every word on the page.
● They choose to read because it brings them enjoyment and satisfaction.
Schools aim to develop these characteristics in every child, and they welcome parents in helping them achieve their goal.

HOW CAN PARENTS HELP?

Schools are responsible for teaching children to read and write. Even the five year old entering the classroom for the first time is likely to have strong expectations about being initiated into the mysteries of print. Sometimes parents of school-age children feel it's best to stand aside now and 'let the school get on with the job'. They worry that they may work against the school if they continue to encourage their children's reading as they did before school. And yet research shows that the home is almost as important as the school in developing children's love of reading and their understanding of the reading process.

The suggestions that follow are designed to help parents to support young readers in positive ways which in no way conflict with current approaches to the teaching of reading.

Continue to read aloud every day

You may think that once children are starting to read for themselves, your role in reading to them is over. This is not the case — reading aloud to them is still vital because it develops their understanding of more complex language patterns, adds to their vocabularies and, of course, maintains their enjoyment of stories.

From about the age of six or seven, listening to longer stories with chapters, a chapter per night, prepares young readers for the tasks involved in following novels for themselves. You can further help by discussing the story from time to time, encouraging your child to keep track of individual characters, the main plot and the interwoven subplots. You can ask children to *tell me what's happened so far* — this requires a form of summarising, of picking out what is important and what detail is less significant. Make it a game where your child starts retelling, then stops at some point from which you must continue. You do so, then hand back to the child, and so forth. It will keep you both on your toes!

The read-aloud time need not be restricted to stories — try some collections of poems. Start with funny ones, for example by Doug Macleod, Spike Milligan, Max Fatchen or Michael Rosen. (You will find many titles suitable for reading aloud in chapter 18.)

Continue to model good reading attitudes

If our children are to value reading, we need to show that it's a priority in our lives too. Regular visits to the library for browsing and borrowing should be as important as soccer training or piano practice.

Aspects of your everyday behaviour that you may take for granted can provide powerful learning experiences for your children. When you turn off the television and curl up with a book, you are saying something about the importance of reading in your own life. When you reach for a dictionary to check a meaning or a spelling, or chase up in the library or concise encyclopedia some interesting point from a television program, you are showing them how reading can serve to achieve many different purposes. You can also encourage children to help you read and follow directions in manuals, recipe books, patterns, craft books and so on.

Often children need to do more than just observe you: they benefit from your talking with them about your own reading. You can read aloud something of interest in the newspaper, or talk about a story which really fascinated you. On library visits you can even demonstrate the process by which you select books — the use of the title and cover, the back-cover blurb, or skimming and scanning a book, are mysteries to many children!

Help your children find time for reading

Many children in the 1990s lead very organised lives. They have less time for just 'messing around with books' because they are so busy going from school to music lesson or gym practice or ballet or sports training or some organised children's activity. By the time they fit in school homework and television viewing, they are too tired to read in bed!

If you believe that reading at home is important, you may need to negotiate with your children some daily time especially set aside for family reading. For example you may allow them to stay awake for an extra half hour, provided they spend it in bed reading. The most efficient way for children to build up reading strategies is to enjoy silent, sustained reading of a book of their own choice every day.

Reading homework

The very best kind of reading homework is the sustained, silent reading described above. Some children are reluctant readers, however. It is often advisable to assist them by setting realistic, achievable goals. For instance, they could aim to read silently for ten minutes, perhaps even using the kitchen timer! The only rules are that children must choose a book they would like to read and know is within their capacity. The only monitoring may be some form of retelling, for example: 'While I put the dishes away, come and tell me about the part you've been reading'.

Encourage reluctant readers to finish the book — even if it takes days — and congratulate them on their success when they have managed to read a book from cover to cover.

What about listening to children read?

We do not make much use of 'oral reading' as a teaching technique these days. Since silent reading is the most natural and efficient way of reading, we prefer to encourage that. In many ways, oral reading is more difficult than silent reading: the reader must focus on every word in sequence, which is not the case in silent reading; and must simultaneously concentrate on using proper phrasing and emphasis to interpret and convey the author's message.

Oral reading is necessary at times in life, but usually for some kind of public performance, and so teachers encourage children to rehearse their oral reading by first reading it silently, then reading it aloud to themselves to work out how to best interpret the piece with their voices. We may sometimes ask children to read aloud a story without any preparation, but this is usually a means of finding out how young readers are going.

Our advice to you is *not* to require children to read aloud unless the teacher specifically requests it. In that case, try to make the experience a meaningful and enjoyable one. Encourage them to read with as few interruptions as possible. When you see that they are flagging, stop and discuss the story. Try to make your stop at a natural point within the story. Children should understand that when you are listening to them read, you are *not* expecting an exact, precise rendition of what's on the page, word for word. You are *not* testing them on their knowledge of words or sounds. You *are*, however, expecting them to gain meaning from what is read.

If children find oral reading a painful task, try the 'You read a paragraph, then I'll read a paragraph' technique. Children seem to enjoy sharing the workload.

Beginning readers, typically children in the first couple of years of school, may feel more comfortable reading aloud because they are still learning that for every word printed on the page there is a spoken equivalent. Matching their voices with the print is one way of practising this learning. The books these beginning readers choose (or are given) to read aloud should be well within their grasp, so that they can make sense, find enjoyment and satisfaction, and gain confidence in their growing competence. Should your youngsters stumble over every second or third word in a book, take it as a sign that the book is inappropriate for this kind of reading. If you want, read it aloud to them.

When should I interrupt?

Your role as listener and helper is a complex one — a mixture of carefully timed intervention and intelligent inactivity. In other words, you need to judge carefully when to interrupt, when to offer help or correction, or when to allow the reader to continue in spite of errors.

You should only interrupt if it becomes obvious that children are not making sense of the text. If the book is too difficult, find a face-saving way of abandoning it. Maybe the 'you read a bit, I read a bit' strategy will work. Perhaps you can read the book aloud while they follow the text.

What if children can't work out an unfamiliar word?

As a rule of thumb, just tell them the word; or if it does not seem very important to overall meaning, simply suggest that they leave it out.

Don't encourage them to sound out the word or break it up into parts as the first strategy. Word-based or sounding-out strategies are only a part of the effective reader's total repertoire of word-solving tactics. They are best left to the school to teach, and used in isolation can distract children from the main task of making sense of the text.

If you do occasionally want to work on strengthening the word-solving strategies of your developing readers, try the following steps:

1   Suggest that children leave out the unfamiliar word and read on, looking for meaning clues to the word in the following text. Stop at a suitable place (usually the end of a sentence).

2   Ask them to go back and reread the sentence with the unfamiliar word, but this time trying to fit in or guess a word that will make sense in the sentence.

3   If the substituted word makes sense, praise children for 'working it out'. If the substitution does not make sense, ask something like: 'Does that sound right, in that sentence?' 'Is that a real word?' 'Does that make sense?' If that gets you nowhere, tell them the word.

If the substituted word makes sense, but is not the exact word used by the author, you may on some occasions go one step further and lead children to combine their knowledge of print (particularly the beginnings and endings of words) with their strategies for making sense. An example might best illustrate the process.
*   The text reads: *When she had the fire burning, she said, 'Who will go and get the kettle filled with water for the spring?'*
*   The word *kettle* is unfamiliar to Matthew. Using the 'leave it out, read on, go back' strategy, he comes up with the substitute *pot*. As a helper, I say, '*Pot* — that really makes sense. That's a good guess. But look, it might be another word that means the same as *pot*.' I cover *kettle* with my thumb, so that Matthew can only see the first letter, *k*. I say, 'Look at the first letter. Can you think of another word that means the same as *pot* — a word for something you put water in to boil — that starts this way?' It's

possible that Matthew may search through his vocabulary and *predict* the word *kettle*. Then we can look at the final letters — they help us *confirm* that it actually is *kettle*. 'Yes, look, it ends the same way as *little*. It must be *kettle*.'

If Matthew does not predict the word, I tell him what it is, of course, without conveying any sense of anger on my part or failure on his.

BOOKS FOR DEVELOPING READERS

What kinds of books are best?

Any text which is meaningful and inherently interesting to the reader is appropriate. Real stories, with interesting plots and characters and rich but natural language, are always preferable to books written only to 'teach children to read'. (For a detailed listing, see chapter 18.)

Don't be surprised if developing readers return again and again to old favourites, or if they get stuck on the one author. Tantalise them with new titles, but don't force them — they will soon want to move on to something new. It is worth remembering also that keen interest in a topic or a breadth of knowledge about it will make reading much easier.

There are two points to note from this. First, it is very unwise to deny children access to a particular book because we think it is too difficult for them — especially if they seem strongly motivated to read that book. Second, where we expect that the ideas or language of a particular book may make it difficult for children, we can achieve a great deal by taking time to build up their knowledge by discussing the pictures or providing other real experiences before they begin to read the book.

Owning books

Avid readers of books also tend to be avid owners of books, so it's good to continue visits to the bookshop. Books make great gifts for special occasions, but they are a pleasant surprise at any time of the year.

IN CONCLUSION

There are two key concepts which developing readers should come to associate with books: *meaning* and *enjoyment*. If home and school can work in harmony to achieve this, then the partnership will indeed be a fruitful one!

CHAPTER 13
Any difficulties?

Vivienne Nicoll

Sometimes, for a combination of complex reasons, something goes wrong in the process of learning to read. If you suspect this is the case with your child, your first step should be to make an appointment to see the teacher. If there is a problem, the school is likely to have special programs to help your child, either within the classroom or on a daily 'withdrawal' basis (see chapter 6 by Mary Anne Wilkie).

This chapter explores three common reading problems, presented as fictional case studies. They are based on scores of real children who have overcome their difficulties in ways similar to those suggested here.

IS THE PROBLEM ONE OF RELUCTANCE?

Stephen, aged 9, is not a very keen reader. Like many children today, he leads a very busy life — there's soccer in winter, cricket in summer, as well as Cubs. And, of course, there's a bit of homework to squeeze in, on top of lots of television viewing. It's easy for him to use lack of time as a reason to avoid reading. His reluctance to read is further reinforced by the lack of reading models he sees at home. Mum actually reads a lot, and she reads to Stephen and his sister every night, but Dad doesn't read much at home, only the weekend newspaper. Stephen is at an age where he identifies strongly with male role models, but the only people he sees enjoying reading are women — his teacher, mother and sister. He thinks reading is 'sissy' and a chore.

What can Stephen's parents do?

- You've probably worked it out for yourself. They need a concerted campaign to help Stephen feel more enthusiastic about books. They will need to change some family behaviour: maybe Dad should read the bedtime story; the television may have to be turned off early each evening, so *everyone* can settle down with a book. They can help Stephen choose material that matches his interests: books and magazines about hobbies, sport or making things; comic books; books that tie in with movies; popular 'series' books.
- There might be a 'contract' between Stephen and his parents, with a reward attached if he keeps his side of the bargain. For example, he might agree to read the book of

his choice silently for fifteen minutes each evening. He could set the kitchen timer and read till the bell rings, then come and tell Dad about what he's read. Dad and Mum's part of the bargain is to match his time: that is, for every fifteen minutes he spends reading, they'll spend fifteen minutes with him in the activity of his choice — kicking a ball around, or working on his model car.

IS THE PROBLEM ONE OF CONFIDENCE?

Connie's Mum is surprised by her daughter's attitude to reading now. Connie loved books before she went to school, but she's been in school just over a year and a half and she doesn't like reading for herself at all, though she still likes to be read to.

What Mum doesn't know is that at some point, Connie became frightened of taking risks with her reading. She had a teacher last year, at her old school, who emphasised getting the 'sounds' right. When Connie said she could already read, she was told that was impossible, because she didn't know all the sounds or words in the book she was given. Now Connie is afraid to predict a word, in case she's wrong. In fact, whenever she reads aloud she keeps stopping after each word and looking to her teacher (or, at home, to her Mum) to see if she's correct. When she comes to an unfamiliar word she just stops in her tracks and won't proceed until someone tells her what it is.

What should Connie's Mum do?

Connie has to learn that it's important to take risks in reading, and that it's not important to read every letter — or even every word — on the page. Her teacher is working on this. She knows what happened to Connie last year, and also that Connie compares herself unfavourably to her older sister, who is a very fluent reader. She has suggested to Connie's Mum some ways she can help.

● Mum can give Connie as much praise as possible and be sure not to compare Connie's reading unfavourably with her sister's. Connie can be praised for little things — having a go at predicting an unfamiliar word or persevering with reading a whole picture book by herself.

● Mum will also put much greater emphasis on Connie's silent reading. For this Connie needs books with which she is already familiar or which are well within her capacity.

● Mum will not expect Connie to read aloud to her, because she realises that in oral reading, accuracy assumes greater importance; 'errors' and difficulties are public and therefore much more obvious.

● Mum is also making tapes of some favourite books for Connie to read along with silently.

IS THE PROBLEM ONE OF MAKING SENSE?

Marc's parents didn't know he had reading problems until the last parent-teacher night. Marc, aged 8, has never liked reading much, but they thought it was just because he was such an active boy. Apparently, Marc hasn't worked out how to use his reading strategies effectively. His teacher says that sometimes he just 'barks at print' or 'word-calls', which means that when he reads aloud, what comes out sounds like a string of unconnected words (some of them are not real words) which sometimes look a little like the words on the page, but which don't make much sense at all. He confuses many little words, like *was* and *saw*. And when he's asked to recall what he's read, he can only remember unconnected fragments of the story. The teacher says that Marc has learnt to get through the words at any cost — even if none of them make sense to him. On top of that, he doesn't effectively use his 'graphophonic knowledge' — that is, what he knows about how the letters of print match up to the sounds of spoken language.

How can Marc's parents help?

It will take a long time, perhaps a year, to get Marc back on track. He is getting some special help in the classroom from a support teacher. She has met Marc's parents and told them how they can help Marc at home.

● Marc needs most of the kinds of help suggested for Stephen and Connie. He can also be helped in other ways. When he is reading with a parent, he needs to be helped to concentrate on the *meaning* of what he reads, not just the words or sounds. His Mum or Dad stop him when what he is reading stops making sense, and ask questions like: 'Does that sound like a real word?' 'Does that word fit the sentence?' 'Does it make sense?' They encourage him to predict unfamiliar words instead of relying on 'sounding out', although they do encourage him to use the clues provided by the word's initial and final letters (see chapter 12).

● Marc learns that sometimes he must stop to go back and correct himself when his reading doesn't make sense, but that he doesn't need to correct 'errors' if the word he guesses *does* make sense. Sometimes his parents help him to tape-record himself reading. He plays back the tape and listens, following the text silently, and stops the tape when he finds a place where he should have corrected himself, but didn't. Over a couple of months the tapes will reveal how much his reading has improved.

● Mum is trying 'echo reading', also known as NIM (the *neurological impress method*). Marc chooses a book (one that is not too difficult) and they read it together, except that Mum reads a little louder and ahead of Marc, so that he is her echo. She tracks her finger smoothly under the print as she reads. Occasionally she lowers her voice and drops out of the reading for a couple of seconds, letting Marc take over. She does this every day for fifteen minutes, for about six to eight weeks. As the teacher says, this method greatly increases fluency and confidence in many children.

● Marc's parents talk a lot with him about what he's read. They help him to retell what he's read afterwards, so he knows that meaning is what's most important.

● They also play some fun reading games with him, sent home by the teacher. In one, called *cloze*, he guesses words left out of a story. In another, *text sequencing*, he brings home a story cut into jumbled strips of one or two sentences, and puts it back together again so that it makes sense.

It is not the place of a book like this one to turn parents into teachers of reading. The teaching of literacy and the diagnosis of reading difficulties are clearly the school's responsibility. However, many problems can be helped enormously when school and home work together.

CHAPTER 14
Writing at home

Helen Hogan

One of my most vivid childhood memories is of a table, of all things. Even now, I think I could describe every mark on it. A large table of scrubbed pine (but long before scrubbed pine became fashionable), it sat squarely in the middle of the kitchen of our home in the South Australian countryside.

The family sat around the table to have meals, to chat, to listen to serials on the radio, to write, to read and to be read to. My sisters and I did our homework at the table as quickly as we could. Then there would be time to read, write stories, play board games and enter magazine competitions. Our mother sat at the table to consult cookery books, compose shopping lists, write letters and share snippets of gossip from the letters that she'd received. Dad spread the newspaper on the table to read it, and wrote business letters there.

What happened around that table had a profound influence on the development of my literacy skills, although I wasn't particularly conscious of that at the time.

WHAT HELPS CHILDREN LEARN TO WRITE?

Modern life seems much more complex. My own son's upbringing will be very different from mine. City life and modern technology will see to that. The paths he takes as he develops literacy skills will be different too. But I think that two of the factors that influenced my literacy development, especially the development of my writing skills, are still as relevant today as they were when I was growing up.

Parents

Parents are powerful role-models. Children tend to learn as much from what adults do as from what they say. My parents wrote often; so I did too. If you would like your children to write freely, be a writing role-model. Let them see you writing letters and notes and lists. Share your writing and ask for comments about it. If what you have written isn't perfectly expressed at your first attempt, so much the better! It's good for children to see that adults, too, often need to improve their writing by revising a first draft.

Talking and reading

Writing does not develop in isolation from other aspects of literacy. Talking and reading both help writing. Make sure that yours is a household where there is a lot of talking and discussion — about daily life, school events, plans for the future, current affairs and so on. Children learn to control and develop their language through talking about ideas and experiences with interested adults.

Reading to, and with, your child also helps develop literacy skills, including writing skills. Make sure there are lots of interesting reading materials in your household. Books written by others are not only fun to share, they also provide models of language, and ideas that may be useful for future writing.

THE WORKPLACE

Children need a suitable place to write at home. While it is not necessary for that place to be isolated and silent, it should be free from the distractions of television and radio noise. Children also need a desk or table which allows them to spread out their books and writing materials. The writing place needs to be well lit; make sure a powerful reading lamp is available so that the desk can be used at night as well as during the day.

Essential equipment

It's my experience that children love furnishing their special writing places with all the things needed for writing. Here is my son's list of essentials:
- pens and pencils of various kinds
- erasers, pencil sharpener, liquid paper
- all sorts of writing paper — notepads, exercise books, a diary, blank and lined paper, decorated notepaper
- coloured paper, cardboard, staples, scissors, glue and cellotape for bookmaking

An important addition to the desktop should be a suitable dictionary. Older children may find it useful to have a thesaurus as well. Any other materials needed for a particular writing task may be borrowed from the family bookshelves or a library.

Machines fascinate children. Typewriters are a great favourite for classroom writing. If you have a typewriter sitting unused in a cupboard somewhere, dig it out and let your children use it. Writing on a word-processor is fun, too, if your family is lucky enough to own a computer.

But beware of cluttering the desk with too many things — remember, you need space to write freely.

A REASON FOR WRITING

Children don't only need a suitable place to write. They also need a reason. One of the things I learnt around the kitchen table all those years ago is that writing is a meaningful and purposeful activity. All homes provide many opportunities for purposeful writing activities. Adults and children may be involved in writing notes, shopping lists, telephone messages, party invitations, captions for photo albums, itineraries for holiday trips... Once parents begin to look for opportunities to provide real-life writing experiences around the home, the list of possibilities grows rapidly.

Become a letter-writing family, instead of relying solely on the telephone. Encourage your child to write to members of the family, and to friends. If younger children find it too daunting to write a full letter, suggest they add a note to the end of a letter you have written. Be on the lookout for opportunities to write away for information; perhaps to a tourist bureau if you are planning a family holiday, or to a government agency for data to help with a project. The great thing about letter writing is that there is usually some sort of reply — and all writers, young or old, love to get a response to what they have written!

HOW MUCH SHOULD I HELP WITH MY CHILD'S WRITING?

This is a question teachers are often asked. It is addressed in chapter 7 of this book, where Jan Turbill outlines how primary schools go about teaching writing in the 1990s. The parent information night that most schools organise at the beginning of the year will provide details about your child's school, and class, writing program. Armed with that knowledge you will be able to provide support if children bring home writing from school to be completed.

Generally, however, there are three principles to keep in mind when you are supporting children's writing development at home.

1   Provide help if they ask for it. Talk over ideas to clarify thinking about storylines. Read draft writing and comment on the things you like about it. Help with spelling, grammar and punctuation if you are asked to. But be a friend rather than a critic; leave final decisions about the writing in the hands of the writer. Sometimes, when you are providing help, there may be opportunities to encourage children towards independence. For example, although it takes longer to help children look up a word in a dictionary than it does to spell it out aloud, in the long run encouraging them to use a dictionary is a more effective course of action.

2   Praise constantly — any piece of draft writing will contain errors, but there will also be many praiseworthy aspects of the writing upon which to focus your attention. Praise the good things about the writing, and the effort that went into producing it. If parents emphasise the positive aspects of their writing, children will be more confident about their developing abilities and more likely to want to write often.

3   Demonstrate that you value your children's writing. Find a prominent place around the house to display written efforts. Tell children, and others, how much you enjoy reading these. Use children's writing as reading material for bedtime stories.

Every day at school your child will be asked to write in some form. There is no doubt that children who can express themselves clearly in words have an advantage. Parents who have a positive attitude towards writing and who take the time to provide meaningful writing experiences at home are contributing significantly to their children's progress. And, hopefully, the family will have had some fun in the process!

CHAPTER 15
Spelling at home

Rona Parker

Every won nose its important too bee able two spell words the write weigh!

While the incorrect spelling above is amusing, it communicates a special message: incorrect spelling can make a piece of writing very difficult to read. When this occurs, effective communication is severely hampered. On the other hand, correct spelling greatly assists the writer in communicating a message most powerfully and effectively.

In our society, being a proficient speller *is* important. Good spelling is regarded as the mark of a 'well-educated' person, and because of this it can affect a child's future opportunities and choices in life.

WHAT CAN PARENTS DO TO HELP?

As a parent you can do much to help your child become a proficient speller.

Shouldn't I leave it to the school?

No. The school day is already very full and besides, there are lots of fun activities and games that you can do at home with your children which will help the school to help them become competent and confident spellers.

Won't spelling activities be boring?

Not if you treat them as fun games, and pleasant occasions for doing things with your children. As spelling is closely linked to reading and writing, many of the following suggestions will also provide great opportunities for using and developing children's reading and writing skills.

All the activities suggested are *meant* to be fun. Because of this they also have the potential to be sanity-savers, as well as improve everyone's spelling!

How should I talk to children about spelling?

Perhaps you have vague memories of your own teachers calling the letter *t*, 'tuh', or the letter *l*, 'l-l-l-l', and are wondering if you should do the same? Please don't.

Enlightened teachers today have discarded this practice. Letters may stand for a variety of sounds in different words, but they only have one name. You will help even very young children enormously by using the correct letter names, so call a *t,* 'tee' and an *l,* 'el'!

SPELLING GAMES AND ACTIVITIES

These can happen almost anywhere, but why not start with...

Spelling in the armchair

You have probably been enjoying books with your children every day, from their early years. If not, it's never too late to start! Make sure your children have some alphabet books in the home collection, or arrange to borrow some from the local library. There are many excellent titles available which will delight both children and adults. Talking through such books together greatly assists in developing children's awareness of letters and words.

Other books also offer opportunities for paying very close attention to the print. As you read, try activities such as looking for more words that begin with the same letter, or finding words that begin the same way as the child's name. However, it is very important to let the book dictate the activity, and *never* let your gentle questions or observations about the text interfere with your child's enjoyment of the book.

Spelling and television

While you may wish to monitor your children's viewing, don't abolish television completely. Instead, make time to watch it together. Even those dreaded commercials can be excellent sources of spelling information, as the product name is always clearly visible and usually comes with a supportive commentary. Advertisements often use invented spellings (for example *quik, sox*) and these also provide discussion points.

Spelling in the lounge room

Crosswords are fun games that focus attention on spelling. There are several crossword books on the market, designed for young children, that begin very simply to help them learn the conventions of crosswords. There is also an ample supply of crosswords for older children. A suitable dictionary can be very useful in helping children check their spelling in crosswords.

When children are quite familiar with crosswords and how they work, why not help them make up a crossword for another family member to try? A good way to begin is to choose a topic and write down all the words that spring to mind. Then comes the task of putting them into a crossword! Squared paper is useful here, as it helps you to see where the words can fit. If you own a computer, you might care to buy a crossword-writing program.

Scrabble is another popular word game that older children can enjoy. A dictionary is again useful, not only as a spelling check, but to assist with the refereeing!

It's a good idea in any case to ensure your children have access to a modern dictionary that *they* can use. The range extends from simple picture dictionaries to adult dictionaries, so choose one to suit the individual, and be prepared to replace it as spelling and reading skills develop. (For specific suggestions see chapter 18.)

Spelling in the kitchen

Wet or cold days are ideal for some of these activities, but you could suggest them at any time. The simple pantry cupboard can be a spelling treasure trove, and you may be surprised at just what it contains! Start the game by asking, for example, 'What can you find in the pantry that begins with the same sound as *jelly?*' or 'What can you find that begins with *j*?' If two or more children are playing this game, suggest they make a list, using either words or pictures, and see how long they can make the list. If they use pictures, you can add the words. When all the possibilities have been exhausted, suggest another letter if they still seem enthusiastic.

Reading recipes is an excellent reading and spelling activity and a fun way to help children become aware of the spelling of abbreviations. Supervise younger children in cooking activities that follow a recipe, and explain what the recipe means. Let them help with the measuring and mixing, even if it does mean more mess! Older children will be able to read and cook with less supervision.

Another everyday spelling task is writing the shopping list. Ask your child to help write the list as you check the supplies. Allow younger spellers to use approximated spellings (just check that you can actually read the list before you reach the shops!) and tell them how to spell the words they ask for (using letter names, of course).

Spelling at the computer

If you have a personal computer, buy your children at least one program that enables them to use their spelling skills, such as a word-processing package or game. Ensure that such a program involves children in spelling for a *real* purpose — say, making up a crossword — rather than simply drilling their spelling.

Spelling on holidays

- Writing postcards provides a natural and enjoyable context for using spelling skills. Depending on their ability, children can dictate the message to Grandma, copy the words or do the writing themselves.
- Travel games can not only promote spelling, but also greatly assist adults to arrive in good shape. As well as I spy and spotto, try games with signs: when passing through shopping centres, for example, keep a tally of the businesses beginning with *a, b, c* and so on; or look for signs containing five letters, six letters and so on. (You will find more ideas in chapter 19.)

By choosing the right moment to suggest these activities, and keeping them fun and informal, you will do a great deal to help your child become a confident and competent speller.

CHAPTER 16
Homework

Andrew Buchan

'Haven't you got any homework?'

How often do you, as a parent, ask that question or one like it? Homework — the setting, doing and marking of it — is foremost in the minds of most parents. They very often judge the quality of the classroom teacher on the criterion of homework: is it set and if so, how much?

IS HOMEWORK A GOOD OR BAD THING?

There is no easy answer to this. Some teachers and some schools prefer to see children reading and writing for enjoyment and interest, or pursuing hobbies with their families. They see the hours after school as a time when children should be free to play by themselves and with others. By giving free rein to their imaginations, living out fantasies and acting out real-life situations, children acquire social skills and learn about life. They discover through play how to relate and react to others and what to do in certain situations.

It is often a time when structured group participation begins, as children join sporting groups and associations such as the Brownies or Cubs. It can also be a time for informal learning, with a variety of activities that parents themselves can initiate.

So why do homework?

Today, many parents (and indeed, the general community) see homework as desirable and demand it of the school, from Kindergarten to Year 6. It is seen as a way to establish a regular pattern of schoolwork outside school hours, to develop behaviour which will be useful at secondary and tertiary level and throughout life.

Good homework gives children reinforcement and practice in skills learnt during the day. As well, it helps to inform you, the parents, of what your children are doing and provides you with an opportunity to assist in their learning.

WHAT IS 'GOOD' HOMEWORK?

Homework should be challenging, interesting and relevant to classroom activities. Ideally, homework should not be done in isolation, but as an extension of schoolwork.

Homework should not be too difficult or unfamiliar. Children need to succeed with homework: it should not be frustrating either for them or their parents. Accordingly homework should not introduce new, unknown activities.

HOW MUCH IS REASONABLE?

Homework should not occupy all of a child's time outside school hours. It is not a child-minding activity. You need to know what homework responsibilities your child has and be aware of your own role in homework. This can usually be established at a parent-teacher meeting early in the year, but if you are uncertain contact your child's teacher and ask.

Homework for children in infants and primary schools should not involve excessive amounts of time. The following would be reasonable:
- Kindergarten to Year 2: 10-30 minutes a day
- Years 3 to 4: 30-45 minutes a day
- Years 5 to 6: up to 60 minutes a day

Children may do more if they wish and you may like to use some of the activities suggested later in this chapter.

HOW CAN I TELL IF HOMEWORK IS GOOD AND WORTHWHILE?

Homework differs from school to school. It may follow a set pattern, with a different subject activity each night — reading on Monday night, spelling on Tuesday night and so on. Or it may be given on a daily basis, with work arising from that day's learning activities.

Some schools give a weekly homework sheet, listing activities which have to be completed by the end of the week. More common in senior primary, this allows children to fit the homework around whatever weekly commitments they or their families have.

Below are just some of the worthwhile literacy activities your child may be asked to do.

Kindergarten to Year 2

Children may:
- Read a book.
- Follow up a book reading by retelling the story to you.
- Illustrate a favourite part of a book and write a caption or a character description.
- Draw and label a picture.
- Help you write the shopping list.
- Write up a recipe they have tried.
- Look in newspapers or magazines for words similar to those in their spelling list.
- Review spelling.
- Find household articles that start with a specific letter or sound.
- Write cards and letters such as invitations, thankyou letters and letters requesting resources for a classroom activity.
- Explain or relate a school event or activity.

Years 3 and 4

Children may:
- Read a book or a chapter from a book.
- Respond in some way to a book: by retelling, writing, illustrating, or making a model.
- Write out and illustrate the final copy of their own story.
- Write for a specific purpose — letters, cards, invitations.
- Interview someone for information.
- Explain an activity undertaken at school that day.
- Consult simple reference books for information.
- Review spelling.
- Complete an individual spelling list.

Years 5 and 6

You would expect to find all the activities suggested for Years 3 and 4, but at a more complex level. For example children may:
- Read newspaper articles and identify the main points.
- Interview a person and write a report, especially one expressing a point of view.
- Write a summary of a news item from radio or television.
- Use an atlas to find places read or heard about.
- Undertake individual research for a unit of schoolwork.

WHAT IF THE TEACHER DOESN'T GIVE HOMEWORK?

If no formal homework is set, there are plenty of worthwhile activities you can encourage or help children to do. Some suggestions follow. They may also be useful as additional activities if children have completed formal homework and still want to do more.
- Encourage children to read and talk.
- Go to your local library as a family — borrow books yourself and encourage children to borrow regularly.
- Read aloud to children (consult the class teacher or the librarian for ideas).
- Encourage discussion about books. Ask children open-ended questions such as:
  'What did you think of the book?'
  'What was it about?'
  'Was it a good read?'
  'Do you have a favourite part you'd like to read to me?'
- As children get older, encourage them to read newspapers. Start with the comic strips. Talk about the headlines. After children have read an article, discuss it and you will soon see their level of understanding.
- What about television? It can be a good source of activities: current affairs can be discussed; places can be found in atlases; comparisons can be made between radio and television. Try to watch programs that are educationally worthwhile. But even serials and dramas can be used as a learning experience: discuss the characters (are

they believable?), the plot, the climax and what keeps you watching.
• Give opportunities to write: shopping lists; thankyou letters to friends and relatives; party invitations; letters to penfriends; letters requesting resources and information for a school topic.
• Cooking is great reading practice and also involves maths when measuring is required.
• Practise reading and maths at the supermarket when you are shopping. Find the best buy, read the specials. Round off amounts and keep a running total as you shop.
• Play word games: 'I'm thinking of a two-syllable word which means...'
• Play educational board games such as Scrabble — not only good for vocabulary development, but also for family cooperation.

HOW CAN I HELP WITH HOMEWORK?

Your role as a parent may be an active one of listening and questioning after hearing a story or discussing a news item, or it may be a more passive one of signing the homework to show that you know it has been done.

You can help by establishing a routine at home. Set a homework time. Provide a work area — ideally a desk in the bedroom, especially for older children. Some children prefer to work at the kitchen table, where help is at hand and opinions can be sought and given. If this works for you, then that's fine.

Apart from these practical considerations, there are other ways to help children with their homework.
• Provide a model — let children see you reading and writing as part of your everyday life.
• Check methods being taught in the classroom, especially in reading, writing, spelling and maths, before showing children 'the way we used to do it at school'.
• Be supportive and encouraging rather than anxious and critical. When asked to comment, temper criticism with praise: 'That's a great idea. Can you think of another way of saying it?'
• Be descriptive with your praise: 'I like the way you used that word'.
• Give children incentives if necessary: 'When you've finished that, why don't we play a game or read a story together?'.
• If children lose interest, investigate the cause. It may be that the homework is too difficult, not challenging enough or inappropriate. It may be that they didn't understand the teacher's instructions. Another thing that discourages children is the lack of feedback: if teachers do not respond to their homework, children learn very quickly that they needn't do it. Whatever the cause, consult the teacher if the problem persists.

Remember, it is what happens in the classroom that is important and this cannot always be judged by the homework given. Finally, always be positive about school and learning, and encourage children in all their endeavours.

CHAPTER 17
Projects

Andrew Buchan & Helen Hogan

'Guess what? I've got a project to do!'

School projects — they seem to have been around for ever. Children can find them a source of great satisfaction — or frustration. Every parent of school-age children has an opinion about them, often positive but sometimes negative. 'We didn't even know she had to do a project until the evening before it was due' — many teachers have heard remarks like that.

Do projects have any educational value? We think so, with a couple of provisos. Do parents have a role to play? Yes. Read on . . .

THE VALUE OF PROJECTS

In the last twenty years enormous advances in technology have set off an 'information explosion'. Now, children can get information from a large number of sources: from technological resources, from the mass media and from publications written specifically for them. This is very different from what most parents remember. Way back then, an adult encyclopedia was often the only resource available and one had to pore over it for hours to extract the required information.

One of the most important tasks for teachers and schools today is to help children develop information skills. We want children to be able to find information using a variety of sources and their related technology. We also want them to be confident in their ability to understand and use information effectively. Properly structured, projects have a valuable role to play here, in giving children an opportunity to practise these skills.

LEARNING HOW TO PROCESS INFORMATION

Every day at school, children are acquiring and processing information in all subject areas, but they are not necessarily conscious that this is what they are doing as they learn. However, there may be times during a school day when the teacher specifically focuses on helping children develop the strategies for processing information. This is often done in cooperation with the school librarian, since it is in the library that most of the school's information resources are found.

In many schools children are encouraged to follow a series of steps to complete an information task — a project. One such series of steps is outlined below, along with some of the key questions that may be asked at each stage of the process.

Clarifying the task

- What is the topic about?
- What do I want to find out?
- Are there any key words or ideas that can give me a starting point?

Finding information

- What do I know about the topic already?
- What do I need to find out?
- What information resources can I use?
- Where can I find them?

Choosing relevant information

- How will I record the information that I've found?
- Is all my information true and relevant?
- Is there anything I should leave out?

Organising information

- Can I organise my information under subheadings?
- Are there any gaps in the information I have?
- Do I need to find visual or aural information?

Presenting information

- With whom do I have to share the information?
- How can I best present my material?

Evaluating the task

- Did I do what I set out to do?
- Did my audience find my information interesting?
- What did I learn about the task that I will be able to use next time?
- Did I enjoy the task?

Of course, no learning task proceeds as simply as the outline above might suggest. Some children may not need to use all the steps. Most children will move backwards and forwards between the steps as they progress through the task. For younger children, the process may need to be simplified. But all children may find the step-by-step plan a useful starting point to help them on their way.

HOW PARENTS CAN HELP

Find out about the school's expectations

At the start of the year most schools have parent information nights and the school's or the teacher's expectations and attitudes concerning projects will probably be explained then. (They may, for instance, be part of the school's homework policy.) If not, however, use the general question and discussion time to ask what will be expected. You may even be able to find out what projects will be set during the year, and some examples of work from the previous year may be available.

When a project is set, your children need to be very clear about what it entails. This may be explained in guidelines sent out by the teacher as part of the project. These guidelines may give a general outline of the work being studied and how the project relates to it. A suggested 'plan of attack' for the project may also have been discussed and distributed. Ideally, this would have been prepared jointly by the teacher and children.

If there are no guidelines, try to get children to tell you what is expected of them. If you are unable to do this and it is obvious that children have no clear direction in mind, then contact the school and ask for help.

Help children choose appropriate material

Parents can play a major role by helping their children choose appropriate material for the information task they are about to undertake. Resources are available from the school library and from the local municipal library.

Children may choose from a variety of materials — reference books, magazines, charts, posters, computer programs, pamphlets, audiocassettes, records, compact discs, videotapes and so on. Encyclopedias are also a useful source of information, but should be used judiciously because the information is often presented in complex language. The list of possible resources grows each year. Very soon, for instance, some children will be able to use modems to tap into worldwide computer information sources (banks).

As well as all this dazzling technology, remember that people are a marvellous resource for some project topics. Children can gain much by interviewing people who are knowledgeable about a particular topic.

Offer some useful techniques

How can information be collected and presented? Children may need help in collecting information from their resources and organising it for presentation in a final project form. The techniques described below will assist with this.

Building a word web. This technique is particularly useful when a broad, general topic has been set. Children should:
- Brainstorm and record all the ideas they can think of that are associated with the topic, including main ideas, dates, places and people.
- Organise these into subheadings around the main topic.

● Link connected ideas together.

A word web for a project about famous Australians and their contribution to Australia's development might look like this:

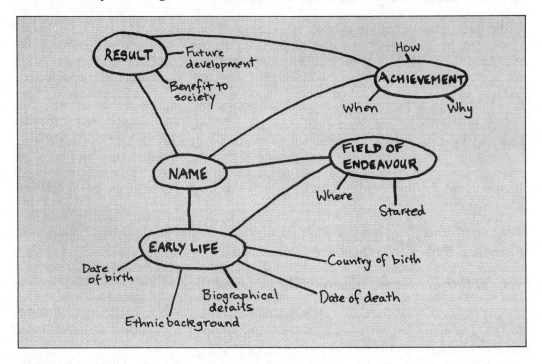

Three-column plan. This technique is useful for getting children to be specific about what information they need to find out. Here, children should:

● Divide a piece of paper into three columns and give the columns the following headings:

What I know

What I want to know

Where I can find this out

● In the first column, list all they know about a project or topic.

● In the second column, list all the questions they want answered.

● Check in the first column and see if there are any answers to questions asked in the second column. If there are, link them by drawing a line.

● Finally, write down in the third column the resources needed to answer the remaining questions in the second column.

Children are now ready to answer the specific questions.

Words in the margin. There is a great temptation simply to copy whole sections from reference books. To help children avoid this practice, here is a technique for finding and recording the main ideas and key words of a text. Children should:

● Slip a single sheet of paper behind the page of the relevant text, leaving about 25mm showing as a margin along the edge of the page.

- Read the passage, paragraph by paragraph. At the end of each paragraph, look for a key word or phrase which is important to the paragraph and write it in the margin beside the paragraph.
- Now turn the phrase into a question and retell as many things as they can remember about the paragraph.
- Check by rereading the paragraph. If necessary, change the key words and repeat the process.
- Finally, make a list of all the words in the margin.

Underlining. If using photocopied material or material that can be written on, children can underline the main ideas or key words in a paragraph. They should:
- Read sentence by sentence, underlining or highlighting the main point in each sentence after reading the whole sentence.
- At the end of the paragraph, review all the underlined or highlighted items, making changes as necessary.
- Make a list of all the key words from each sentence.

Help with a project plan

When all the information has been collected, the project needs final planning for presentation. The following technique is useful for material that contains headings and subheadings, diagrams and other aids. Children should:
- On the left-hand side of a blank piece of paper, write the main headings. (These will vary in number from child to child.)
- Beside each main heading, list subheadings linked to the main heading.
- Beside the subheading, on the right-hand side of the paper, list any supporting aids such as graphs, photographs, diagrams and illustrations. Show the links with lines.
- Redraft if necessary.
- To complete the project, write a paragraph for each subheading and include the appropriate aids. Then write a brief introduction and conclusion.

Suggest ideas for presentation

Projects are traditionally presented in a special project book, or on a sheet of cardboard, procured from the local newsagent. If cardboard is going to be used, give some thought to planning. Help your children plan the setting out, the borders, the heading and the layout of their work.

To overcome the problem of correcting errors on the cardboard, children might complete the writing, illustrations, diagrams and maps on sheets of paper and paste these on to the cardboard.

Alternatively, how about a different method of presentation? Perhaps a model or a diorama would be appropriate. Perhaps it would be possible to present all the information as a taped interview. Or how about a play? Really, the method of presentation is limited only by one's imagination.

We hope you can use some of these ideas to help your children along the way. It may take time to get them started, but resist the temptation to take over the project yourself. You might get better marks, but children need to learn the skills of independent inquiry and research for themselves. Properly managed, projects can be a rewarding educational experience.

Good luck!

Acknowledgment

In preparing this chapter, the authors found the following publication particularly useful: *Information Skills in the Classroom* (NSW Department of School Education, 1990).

CHAPTER 18
Building a family book collection

Vivienne Nicoll & Victoria Roberts

BEG, BORROW OR BUY BOOKS!

People who read for pleasure and leisure have a strong urge to own books. This collection of books need not be large, but it should include children's favourite stories and poetry, information books and some reference materials.

Most families borrow the bulk of what they read — from their school, friends, playgroup or local library. From the earliest age, however, children can learn the value of books by owning them. Birthdays, Christmas and other special occasions are obvious times to purchase books as gifts, but any excuse will do! For instance if your child borrows a book from the library and is loath to return it, this might be the ideal opportunity for a worthwhile surprise present.

A specialist children's bookshop will have the largest range of books, but if you are not near one, befriend your local bookseller. Many preschools and schools make use of commercial bookclubs whereby children can purchase regularly from a selection of titles appropriate to their age group. Variety stores and supermarkets often offer books at very low prices; sometimes you will find a gem, but beware of 'formula-written' books with poor-quality paper and second-rate illustrations. They generally offer little challenge and are unlikely to be revisited or become favourites.

The suggestions that follow provide general guidelines for building a family book collection which should grow with your child from birth to secondary school. As space is limited here, and as thousands of new titles are published every year, we recommend that you consult any of the book guides listed in the Bibliography (p. 94).

FROM BIRTH TO FIVE YEARS OLD

If you make the effort to read with your children, they will develop an interest in books long before they can hold a book for themselves. Books should have the same status as toys; reading should become part of play and a familiar activity in their day. Although at this age most of children's reading will be done by an adult, you can encourage their participation by talking about the book as you read and responding to their queries, comments and enjoyment. As your children's familiarity with books grows you may notice 'reading-like' behaviour: reading to Teddy; talking to themselves while turning the pages of a book.

Essential reading — choose books from each of the following categories.

- A nursery-rhyme anthology, such as one of the following:

Raymond Briggs, *The Mother Goose Treasury*, Puffin, Penguin Books.
Tomie de Paola, *Tomie de Paola's Mother Goose*, Methuen.
Charlotte Voake, *Over the Moon: A Book of Nursery Rhymes*, Walker Books.
Margaret Tarrant, *Children's Verse*, Tiger.
Iona & Peter Opie, *The Puffin Book of Nursery Rhymes*, Puffin, Penguin Books.

- A small assortment of board books (0-3 years), preferably with text:

Moira Kemp, *Round and Round the Garden, Knock at the Door* and others, Five Mile Press.
Fiona Pragoff, *Growing; Opposites* and *How Many?*, Gollancz.
Bob Graham, *Playing; Waking* and *Sleeping* (Busy Day series), Five Mile Press.

- Alphabet and counting books:

John Burningham, *ABC*, Jonathan Cape.
Brian Wildsmith, *ABC* and *123*, Oxford University Press.
Robert Crowther, *The Most Amazing Hide-and-Seek Alphabet Book*, Viking Kestrel.
Jan Ormerod, *Joe Can Count*, Walker Books.
Eric Carle, *1, 2, 3 To the Zoo*, Puffin, Penguin Books.
John Brennan, *1, 2, 3 And What Do You See?*, Dent.

- Concept books, for example:

Rod Campbell, *The Noisy Book*, Lothian (environmental sounds).
Allan & Janet Ahlberg, *The Baby's Catalogue*, Puffin, Penguin Books (family life).
Shiego Watanabe, *How Do I Put It on?*, Puffin, Penguin Books (getting dressed).
John Prater, *On Friday Something Funny Happened*, Puffin, Penguin Books (days of the week).
Tracey Lewis, *Eye Spy*, Golden Press (colours).
My First Look at Sizes and other titles in the series, Reader's Digest.

- Wordless picture books which tell a story:

Jan Ormerod, *Sunshine* and *Moonshine*, Puffin, Penguin Books.
Pat Hutchins, *Changes, Changes*, Bodley Head.
Donald Crews, *Truck*, Bodley Head.

- Collections of verse, rhyme and song:

Jill Bennett, *Days Are Where We Live and Other Poems*, Bodley Head; and *Tiny Tim: Verses for Children*, Picture Lions, Collins.
Jack Prelutsky, *The Walker Book of Read-aloud Rhymes for the Very Young*, Walker Books.
Sarah Hayes, *Stamp Your Feet Action Rhymes*, Heinemann.
Pie Corbett, *The Kingfisher Playtime Treasury*, Kingfisher.
Dorothy Butler, *For Me, Me, Me*, Hodder & Stoughton.

- Books with flaps, cut-outs or pop-ups:

Eric Hill, *Where's Spot?* (and other Spot titles), Puffin, Penguin Books.
Maureen Roffey, *Home Sweet Home*, Piper, Pan Books.
Colin & Jacqui Hawkins, *Old Mother Hubbard*, Magnet Books.
Janet & Allan Ahlberg, *Peepo!*, Puffin, Penguin Books.
Carol Jones, *Old Macdonald Had a Farm*, Angus & Robertson.

- Books where children can join in with the reader:

Eric Carle, *The Very Hungry Caterpillar*, Puffin, Penguin Books.
Elfrida Vipont, *The Elephant and the Bad Baby*, Puffin, Penguin Books.
Lynley Dodd, *Hairy Maclary from Donaldson's Dairy*, Puffin, Penguin Books.
Janet & Allan Ahlberg, *Each Peach Pear Plum*, Picture Lions, Collins.
Ron Maris, *Better Move On, Frog!*, Picture Lions, Collins.
Jack Kent, *The Fat Cat*, Puffin, Penguin Books.

John Burningham, *Mr Gumpy's Outing*, Puffin, Penguin Books.
Bill Martin, Jr, *Brown Bear, Brown Bear, What Do You See?*, Picture Lions, Collins.
Rod Campbell, *Dear Zoo*, Puffin, Penguin Books.
Pat Hutchins, *Good-night, Owl!*, Puffin, Penguin Books.
Quentin Blake, *Mr Magnolia*, Picture Lions, Collins.
Thomas & Wanda Zachariah, *But Where is the Green Parrot?*, Piccolo.
Franz Brandenburg, *Cock-a-doodle-do*, Picture Piper, Pan Books.
Ruth Brown, *A Dark, Dark Tale*, Puffin, Penguin Books.
Pamela Allen, *Who Sank the Boat?*, Nelson.
Mem Fox, *Hattie and the Fox*, Aston Scholasitc.
- Information books: any title by Byron Barton, e.g. *Machines at Work*, Julia MacRae.

THE FIRST YEARS OF SCHOOL

Children of this age are gaining confidence as readers. As they solve the puzzle of print they will want to read for themselves more and more. This does not mean the end of your role in reading to and with them. It is important that you still read aloud to your children, especially old favourites and more challenging books that they may not yet be able to read for themselves. The books that they do read for themselves may be shorter, with fairly predictable text, natural language and lots of supportive illustrations. Don't worry if for a time they become hooked on a series of books about the same character or theme — these familiar elements allow them to experience success and to consolidate their literacy skills.

As school, sporting and leisure activities begin to crowd the child's day it is important to establish some time to read, for instance before bed, instead of watching television or during family time on the weekend.

As children's confidence grows, their appetite for books may become insatiable. You will need to borrow books regularly from school and local libraries, which will allow you to be very selective about your book purchases.

The following categories offer starting points for selection.
- Rich retellings of folktales and fairytales, for example:
The Walker Fairy Tale Library, Walker Books (twelve paperback books, each containing at least three stories).
Virginia Haviland, *The Fairy Tale Treasury*, Puffin, Penguin Books.
Helen Oxenbury, *The Helen Oxenbury Nursery Story Book*, Heinemann.

There are also many picture-book versions of individual tales by authors like Susan Jeffers, Errol Le Cain, Paul Galdone, William Stubbs, Arlene Mosel, Verna Aardema, Bernadette Watts and Lisbeth Zwerger.
- Australian Aboriginal stories, especially those told by or collected from Aboriginal people, e.g. Dick Roughsey, Pamela Lofts.
- Picture books for joining in:
Raymond Briggs, *Jim and the Beanstalk*, Puffin, Penguin Books.
Roald Dahl, *The Enormous Crocodile*, Puffin, Penguin Books.
Jill Murphy, *Peace at Last*, Macmillan.
Mem Fox, *Possum Magic*, Omnibus.
Judith Viorst, *Alexander and the Terrible, Horrible, No Good, Very Bad Day*, Angus & Robertson.
Janet & Allan Ahlberg, *Funnybones*, Picture Lions, Collins.

Babette Cole, *Princess Smartypants*, Picture Lions, Collins.
Esphyr Slobodkina, *Caps For Sale*, Scholastic.
Amanda Graham, *Arthur*, Era.
Ruth Brown, *The Big Sneeze*, Andersen Press.
Libby Handy, *Boss For a Week*, Ashton Scholastic.
Gerald Rose, *Trouble in the Ark*, Ashton Scholastic.
John Burningham, *The Shopping Basket*, Picture Lions, Collins.
● Picture books for thinking about:
Jenny Wagner, *John Brown, Rose and the Midnight Cat*, Puffin, Penguin Books.
Tomie de Paola, *Oliver Button Is a Sissy*, Magnet.
Verna Aardema, *Why Mosquitoes Buzz in People's Ears*, Dial Press.
Anthony Browne, *Willy the Wimp; Willy the Champ* and *Gorilla*, Magnet.
John Burningham, *Borka*, Puffin, Penguin Books.
Martin Waddell, *Can't You Sleep, Little Bear?*, Little Mammoth, Octopus.
Aliki, *Feelings*, Piccolo.
Tony Bradman & Joanna Burroughes, *Not Like That, Like This!*, Beaver Books.
● Books for parents to share over a number of sittings:
Janet & Allan Ahlberg, *Jeremiah in the Dark Woods*, Viking Kestrel.
Jill Tomlinson, *The Owl Who was Afraid of the Dark*, Puffin, Penguin Books.
Robin Klein, *Thing* and *Thingnapped*, Oxford University Press.
Jeff Brown, *Flat Stanley*, Magnet.
Roald Dahl, *George's Marvellous Medicine*, Puffin, Penguin Books.
Michael Bond, the Paddington Bear stories, Lions, Collins.
Morris Lurie, *The 27th Annual African Hippopotamus Race*, Puffin, Penguin Books.
E. B. White, *Charlotte's Web*, Puffin, Penguin Books.
● Poetry:
Clare Scott-Mitchell, *When a Goose Meets a Moose*, Methuen.
June Factor, *Big Dipper* (and others in the series), Oxford University Press.
Jill Bennett, *Roger Was a Razorfish*, Bodley Head.
Jack Prelutsky (ed.), *The Walker Book of Poetry for Children*, Walker Books.
Barbara Ireson, *Rhyme Time* and *Rhyme Time 2*, Beaver Books.
● Books for children to read. There are various series which fulfil children's need for books to practise upon as their reading skills develop, for example:
Cat on the Mat books (various titles and authors), Oxford University Press.
Hello Reading (various titles and authors), Puffin, Penguin Books.
Allan Ahlberg & Colin McNaughton, Red Nose Readers (various titles), Walker Books.
● Information books: as children's knowledge of the world grows, they want to find out more about different topics. Help them to explore the non-fiction section of the library. They will often choose titles beyond their current reading capacity, so they will need your help to read them. When your child shows an avid interest in a topic you may decide to purchase rather than borrow from the library.

THE MIDDLE YEARS

During the middle years you may notice considerable growth in children's reading, both in competence and confidence. It is during this period that most children learn to make sense of the words without relying on pictures for clues. They also begin to develop reading 'stamina': that is, they can sustain reading for a greater length of time and can read a longer text, such as a short chaptered story, over a number of occasions.

As children experience a variety of books, different in style, theme and format, they begin to develop an individual taste in books and can justify their selection of particular titles. This taste will be reflected in their library borrowing and purchases.

Although children in the middle years can read for themselves, they still need an attentive and enthusiastic adult reading partner with whom to discuss stories; someone to read them longer, more challenging stories that they can return to independently in future years. Suggested starting points follow.

● Junior novels: short, chaptered stories, usually with some pictures and largish print. A feature of readers in this age group is that they particularly enjoy reading 'series' titles which involve recurring characters. Titles marked with an **S** belong to this category.

Florence Parry Heide, *The Shrinking of Treehorn*, Puffin, Penguin Books.
Eleanor Coerr, *Sadako and the Thousand Paper Cranes*, Hodder & Stoughton.
Beverly Cleary, *Ramona The Pest*, Puffin, Penguin Books (**S**).
Gillian Rubinstein, *Melanie and the Night Animal*, Puffin, Penguin Books.
Emily Rodda, *Something Special* and *Pigs Might Fly*, Puffin, Penguin Books.
Christobel Mattingley, *Duck Boy*, Golden Press.
Robin Klein, *The Enemies*, Golden Press; and *Junk Castle*, Oxford University Press.
Osmar White, *The Super Roo of Mungalongaloo*, Puffin, Penguin Books (**S**).
Jill Murphy, *The Worst Witch*, Puffin, Penguin Books. (**S**).
Margaret Stuart Barry, *Simon and the Witch*, Lion, Collins. (**S**).
Judy Blume, *Freckle Juice*, Heinemann Chimps; and *Tales of a Fourth Grade Nothing*, Piccolo, Pan Books (**S**).
Roger McGough, *The Great Smile Robbery*, Puffin, Penguin Books.
Joan Phipson, *Hide Till Daytime*, Puffin, Penguin Books.
Pat Hutchins, *Follow That Bus*, Young Lions, Collins (**S**).
Ted Hughes, *The Iron Man*, Faber & Faber.
Roald Dahl, *The BFG*, Puffin, Penguin Books.
Trevor Todd, *Old Sam, Jasper and Mr Frank*, Puffin, Penguin Books.
Doris Buchanan Smith, *A Taste of Blackberries*, Puffin, Penguin Books.
Diana Kidd, *Onion Tears*, Collins.
Nance Donkin, *The Best of the Bunch*, Ashton Scholastic.
Barbara Giles, *Bicycles Don't Fly*, Puffin, Penguin Books.
Michael Dugan, *The Great Overland Riverboat Race*, Puffin, Penguin Books.
Max Dann, *Ernest Pickle's Remarkable Robot*, Oxford University Press.
S. A. Wakefield, *Bottersnikes and Gumbles*, Puffin, Penguin Books.
Shirley Hughes, *Chips and Jessie*, Young Lions, Collins.

● Picture books:
Nadia Wheatley & Donna Rawlins, *My Place*, Collins Dove.
Anthony Browne, *Hansel and Gretel* and *The Tunnel*, Julia MacRae.
John Burningham, *Come Away From the Water, Shirley* and *Time to Get Out of the Bath, Shirley*, Picture Lions, Collins; *Granpa*, Puffin, Penguin Books.
Michael Foreman, *War and Peas*, Puffin, Penguin Books.
Laurene Krasny Brown & Marc Brown, *Visiting an Exhibition*, Collins.
Taro Yashima, *Crow Boy*, Puffin, Penguin Books.
Lydia Pender, *The Useless Donkeys*, Methuen.
Brian Wildsmith, *Professor Noah's Spaceship*, Oxford University Press.
Margaret Wild & Julie Vivas, *The Very Best of Friends*, Margaret Hamilton.
Russell Hoban, *How Tom Beat Captain Najork and His Hired Sportsmen*, Jonathan Cape.

- Collections of short stories:

Ted Hughes, *How the Whale Became and Other Stories*, Puffin, Penguin Books.
Ted Greenwood, *Ginnie*, Viking Kestrel.
Margaret Mahy, *The Great Piratical Rumbustification* and *The Chewing-Gum Rescue and Other Stories*, Puffin, Penguin Books.
Joan Aiken, *A Necklace of Raindrops*, Puffin, Penguin Books.

- Traditional literature (folktales, fairytales, myths, legends and hero tales):

Sara & Stephen Corrin (eds), *The Faber Book of Modern Fairy Tales*, Faber & Faber.
Hans Christian Andersen, *Michael Hague's Favourite Hans Christian Andersen Fairy Tales*, Methuen.

- Poetry: hardback anthologies of poetry make good gifts for special occasions; shorter paperback collections are good to add to the home collection too. Don't forget the poetry shelves of the library.

Clare Scott-Mitchell, *Apples From Hurricane Street*, Methuen.
Jill Heylen & Celia Jellett, *Someone is Flying Balloons*, Omnibus.
Beatrice Schenk de Regniers, *Sing a Song of Popcorn*, Ashton Scholastic.
Michael Rosen, *Mind Your Own Business* and *Don't Put Mustard in the Custard*, Picture Lions, Collins; *Quick, Let's Get Out of Here*, Puffin, Penguin Books.
June Factor, *Far Out, Brussel Sprout!* (and others in the series), Oxford University Press.

- Information books: again, be guided by your children's interests and be prepared to help them read more difficult books. A series they may be able to manage for themselves: Eyewitness Guides (various titles and authors), Collins/Angus & Robertson.
- Books for parents to read aloud. Although some children in this age group are ready to read longer novels independently, most will find them easier in the upper primary years. Parents can pave the way by reading longer novels aloud in serial form. Some appropriate titles are listed below, in 'The upper years', and are marked with an **R**.

THE UPPER YEARS

By the last years of primary school, most children have developed into independent readers. Being able to read is one thing; wanting to is another. Parents, then, need to continue the partnership role, giving books a high priority in the home, reading to and with their children, helping them find time for reading and encouraging them to borrow and buy books.

This is often a time when tastes may become set or even faddish. Don't worry — reading fads usually pass, and at least the children are reading. The most positive step is to keep offering alternatives, but in a subtle and non-judgmental way. As they move towards abstract thinking, older children are able to cope with books which are more complex in theme or which require them to take a stance on an issue.

Titles marked with a **P** are suitable for parents to read and discuss with their children.

- Novels:

Katherine Paterson, *Bridge To Terabithia*, Puffin, Penguin Books (**P**).
Lois Lowry, *Anastasia Krupnik*, Lions, Collins (**S, P**).
Gillian Rubinstein, *Space Demons* (**P**) and *Answers to Brut* (**R**), Puffin, Penguin Books.
Robin Klein, *Hating Alison Ashley* and *Boss of the Pool* (**P**), Puffin, Penguin Books; *Penny Pollard's Diary* (**S**), Oxford University Press.

Thurley Fowler, *The Green Wind*, Rigby (**P**).
Libby Gleeson, *Eleanor Elizabeth*, Puffin, Penguin Books.
Judith Kerr, *When Hitler Stole Pink Rabbit*, Lions (**P, S**).
Joan Phipson, *Watcher in the Garden*, Puffin, Penguin Books.
Gene Kemp, *The Turbulent Term of Tyke Tiler*, Puffin, Penguin Books (**P**).
Simon French, *Cannily, Cannily*, Puffin, Penguin Books (**P**).
Nina Bawden, *Carrie's War*, Puffin, Penguin Books (**S**).
Betsy Byars, *The Pinballs* and *The Eighteenth Emergency*, Puffin, Penguin Books.
Beverly Cleary, *Dear Mr Henshaw*, Puffin, Penguin Books.
Russell Hoban, *The Mouse and His Child*, Puffin, Penguin Books.
Margaret Mahy, *The Haunting*, Magnet (**P**).
Eleanor Spence, *The Leftovers*, Ashton Scholastic (**R**).
Randolph Stow, *Midnite*, Puffin, Penguin Books (**R**).
Jenny Wagner, *The Nimbin*, Puffin, Penguin Books (**R**).
Aidan Chambers, *The Present Takers*, Magnet (**P**).
Allan Baillie, *Little Brother*, Puffin, Penguin Books (**P**).
Ruth Park, *Playing Beatie Bow*, Puffin, Penguin Books.
Mordecai Richler, *Jacob Two-Two Meets the Hooded Fang*, Puffin, Penguin Books (**R**).
Philippa Pearce, *Tom's Midnight Garden*, Puffin, Penguin Books.
Patricia Wrightson, *A Little Fear* and *I Own the Racecourse* (**P**), Puffin, Penguin Books.
Nicholas Fisk, *Antigrav*, Puffin, Penguin Books.
Victor Kelleher, *Master of the Grove*, Penguin Books.
Colin Thiele, *Storm Boy*, Rigby (**R**).
Louise Fitzhugh, *Harriet the Spy*, Lions, Collins (**P**).
Robert O'Brien, *The Silver Crown*, Lions, Collins.
Lynne Reid Banks, *The Indian in the Cupboard*, Lions, Collins.
Cynthia Voigt, *Homecoming*, Lions, Collins (**P**).
- Collections of short stories:
David McRobbie, *Flying With Granny and Other Stories*, Heinemann.
Jan Mark, *Nothing to Be Afraid Of*, Puffin, Penguin Books.
Michael Rosen, *Hairy Tales and Nursery Crimes*, Andre Deutsch.
Paul Jennings, *Unreal!; Uncanny!; Unbelievable!* and *Quirky Tales*, Puffin, Penguin Books.
- Traditional literature:
Maurice Saxby & Robert Ingpen, *The Great Deeds Of Superheroes* and *The Great Deeds of Heroic Women*, Millenium.
Kevin Crossley-Holland & Charles Keeping, *Beowulf*, Oxford University Press.
- Picture books — while the novel is a good vehicle for exploring ideas, recent years have seen the rise of the sophisticated picture book for older readers:
Fiona French, *Snow White in New York*, Oxford University Press.
Ian McEwan & Roberto Innocenti, *Rose Blanche*, Jonathan Cape.
Jorg Muller & Jorg Steiner, *The Sea People*, Victor Gollancz.
Junko Morimoto, *My Hiroshima*, Collins.
Alfred Noyes & Charles Keeping, *The Highwayman*, Oxford University Press.
Graeme Base, *Animalia*, Viking O'Neil.
Christobel Mattingley & Marianne Yamaguchi, *The Miracle Tree*, Hodder & Stoughton.
Mitsumasa Anno, *Anno's Journey*, Bodley Head.
- Poetry: Jill Heylen & Celia Jellett, *Rattling in the Wind*, Omnibus.
- Information books: as for the middle years; and try the numerous factual titles by publishers such as Macmillan Australia, Franklin Watts, Wayland and so on.

EXPERIENCING LIFE THROUGH BOOKS

Many of the books recommended in the lists above will satisfy children's delight in humour and fantasy. Others focus more on contemporary, 'realistic' settings and happenings. As children grow older, they experience the pain as well as the joy of living, and the books they read should reflect this. We are fortunate today to have children's authors who tackle issues such as illness, disabilities, family crises and death, with sensitivity and integrity. The best of their books do not offer trite or easy solutions to life's problems, but do always provide in their endings a sense of hope and a celebration of the indomitable human spirit.

While these books can be read at any time, they may be of special significance when children are faced with particular crises in their own lives. A book, however good, cannot take the place of a caring adult-child relationship, but it can be a solace, and also the ideal catalyst for discussion. For appropriate books, we suggest you consult your local children's librarian or specialist bookseller.

THE REFERENCE COLLECTION

In adult life many of us take reference books for granted, because they have become so much a part of our daily life. We go to a dictionary to check the spelling of a word, or the meaning of a word unfamiliar or unclear to us. If writing is part of our work, or if we are involved in study, we frequently find a thesaurus a useful tool. Less frequently we need to refer to an encyclopedia or an atlas.

It is never too early to introduce children to the important role of these reference books, provided the books chosen for them meet their current needs and are replaced as these needs change. As they grow, 'looking it up' should become a useful adjunct to learning. We recommend ownership of a good Australian dictionary and a thesaurus, particularly in the middle and upper years of primary school. A good junior atlas will also be necessary. (Titles marked with an **A** are published in Australia.)

We do not recommend the purchase of a large and expensive set of encyclopedias for the family. The information in these volumes dates very quickly, making them less useful year by year. Also, the encyclopedia sets marketed door-to-door in Australia are usually published in the USA, and lack information with relevance to Australia, or an Australian perspective.

Your children will be taught to use encyclopedias in the school library, and you can encourage them to also make use of those in the local library. You may like to consider the purchase of a one- or two-volume encyclopedia (preferably published in Australia), provided that you replace it with a more recent edition every three years or so. Those listed below vary considerably in length and price, so we suggest that you look carefully at two or three of them before making your choice.

From birth to five years old

• While very young children obviously are not yet ready for dictionaries, you can introduce them to a good 'look-it-up book', one with many labelled pictures of objects from their everyday experience. In some of these books the content is divided into different sections — a good introduction to the way humans attempt to categorise information in books.

Anne James, *One Day: A Very First Dictionary*, Oxford University Press (**A**).
Anne Rockwell, *Things That Go* and *Things to Play With*, E. P. Dutton.
Eric Hill, *Spot's Big Book of Words*, Heinemann.
Richard Scarry, *My Biggest First Book Ever*, Collins.
Paul Strickland, *A Child's First Book of Things*, Five Mile Press (**A**).

The first years of school

- Dictionaries:

My Macquarie Picture Dictionary, Jacaranda Wiley (**A**).
Diane Snowball, *My Picture Dictionary*, Oxford University Press (**A**).
The Young Person's Picture Dictionary, Longman.
The Puffin First Picture Dictionary, Penguin Books.
Collins Picture Dictionary, Collins.

The middle and upper years

- Dictionaries and thesauruses (titles are grouped in ascending order of complexity):

Diane Snowball & Robyn Green, *First Dictionary*, Oxford University Press (**A**).
My First Macquarie Junior Dictionary, Jacaranda Wiley (**A**).
My First Macquarie Junior Thesaurus, Jacaranda Wiley (**A**).
The Macmillan First Thesaurus, Macmillan.
The Macquarie Junior Dictionary, Jacaranda Wiley (**A**).
The Macquarie Junior Thesaurus, Jacaranda Wiley (**A**).
The Australian Primary Dictionary, Oxford University Press (**A**).
The Oxford Children's Thesaurus, Oxford University Press.

- One- or two-volume encyclopedias:

Macmillan Australia Children's Encyclopedia, vols 1 & 2, Macmillan (**A**).
The Guinness Encyclopedia, Collins — for upper primary years, with parental guidance.
Junior Pears Encyclopaedia, Pelham Books — useful with parental guidance.
The Illustrated Family Encyclopedia, Golden Press.
The Penguin Australian Encyclopaedia, Penguin Books — for upper primary years, with parental guidance (**A**).
John Paton (ed.), *The New Concise Children's Encyclopedia*, Bay Books — for middle and upper primary children (**A**).
David Macaulay, *The Way Things Work*, Reader's Digest — a reference book on all things technological.

- Atlases:

The Macquarie Children's Atlas, Jacaranda Wiley (**A**).
The Macmillan Australian Atlas, Macmillan (**A**).
Peter Wilson & John Fien, *The Young Australia Atlas*, Nelson (**A**).
Collins Australian Junior Atlas, Collins (**A**).

Apart from a 'school' or 'student' atlas that can be carried easily in the schoolbag, you may think about buying one of the following for the family collection:

The Times Atlas of the World (Family Edition), Bay Books.
The Macquarie Illustrated World Atlas, Macquarie Library (**A**).

CHAPTER 19
Language learning goes on holiday

Vivienne Nicoll

No more pencils, no more books, no more teachers' dirty looks!

At the end of the school year, the weeks and weeks of holiday stretch ahead. However, holiday time doesn't have to mean an end to reading or writing or imaginative language play. We hope the suggestions for children below will provide you with some terrific ways of insuring your youngsters against holiday boredom, while also supporting positively and painlessly their language development. Some of the ideas can be pursued by children alone, but many will be much more fun if family members try them together.

If you are going away for your holidays, read this through beforehand, as some of the ideas may require you to pack a few additional items.

WRITING

Ask the children if they would like to:
- Write a thankyou letter to Santa Claus, and post it to him care of Australia Post.
- Make and post your own Christmas thankyou cards or notes.
- Make and send your own holiday postcards — paint or draw the scenes on the front, and cut the edge of the cardboard with crimping scissors. Write fun messages on the back.
- Buy a cheap scrapbook and write a diary of your holiday, a page a day, illustrating it with drawings and leaving spaces for holiday photos when they're developed. You might take it to school next year, to share with your friends.
- Buy an exercise book and write the first draft of your own novel, in chapters. Or write the story of your life, including all your most memorable experiences.
- At the beach, write in the firm wet sand with your finger or a stick and exchange messages with your Mum or Dad, sister, brother or friend.

READING

Ask the children if they would like to:
- Go to the local library and borrow some fantastic books to read when it's too hot or too wet, or when you feel too lazy to play.

- Reread some of your old favourites (Roald Dahl, Betsy Byars, Robin Klein...?). Or ask Mum or Dad what their favourite childhood books were and read them.
- Borrow and read some funny poetry books, some exciting fairytales or some factual books about your favourite topics.
- Borrow a craft book and try some of the ideas in it.
- Follow up your holiday with books which help you identify your collections or the interesting things you've seen — seashells, fish, birds, native plants.
- Ask Mum or Dad to buy a good first-aid manual (perhaps the St John's Ambulance one) and study it together.

GAMES TO PLAY

Travelling games

While travelling in the car or coach, the family could play...

I spy with my little eye. You may vary the rules, for example by specifying only items inside the vehicle.

What am I? Try making up riddles like this one: 'I'm liquid. I'm light-coloured. Without me you couldn't go on this trip. I begin with *p*. What am I?'

Categories — a memory game which also involves classifying skills and knowledge of the alphabet. Players take it in turns to build up a list, in alphabetical order. For example:
    Person 1: 'I went to the fruit shop and I bought apples'
    Person 2: 'I went to the fruit shop and I bought apples and bananas'
    Person 3: 'I went to the fruit shop and I bought apples and bananas and cherries'
The next item begins with *d*...and so on. If you get the order wrong, or can't think of a new item with the right initial, you're out until the next round. There are endless permutations, for example:
    'Down by the seaside I saw an albatross, a barnacle, a crab...'
    'As I crept through the jungle I saw an alligator, a bat,...'
    'On our bushwalk I saw an ant, a bandicoot,...' and so on.
There are also variations of the game:
- Use the *same initial letter* only: 'I went to the fruit shop and I bought apples, apricots, avocados, asparagus...' and so on.
- Each person takes as the starting point the *last letter* of the word in the previous turn. For example:
    Person 1: 'As I crept through the jungle I saw a tiger'
    Person 2: 'As I crept through the jungle I saw a rhinoceros'
    Person 3: '...a snake'
    Person 4: '...an elephant'...and so on.

Numberplate games. There are lots of these. For example:
- Keep a list of all the numberplates which make real words.

- Look for numberplates whose letters can be rearranged to make real words.
- Keep a count of interstate numberplates.
- Make up phrases to fill out numberplate letters:
  NSI — Next Stop Icecreams!
  MDD — My Dog's Dirty!

Spotto is simple. You can nominate a category for everyone to spot, for example 'Spotto the red cars' (black cows, dams, police stations or whatever). Alternatively, take it in turns to issue the challenge: 'Spotto something beginning with ...' The person who spots the object has the next turn.

Retellings (the moving finger game). Choose a well-known fairytale. The first person begins to retell it, then stops and points to someone else, who must continue the story from where it was left off, but then may point to someone else — and so on. Alternatively, play the game making up an original story.

Indoor games and activities

At night, or on a wet day, try some alternatives to television...

Charades — a mime game where players act out titles, famous sayings and so on. You know — 'TV show — three words. First word — two syllables. First syllable...'

Homemade theatre — dress up and create your own play.

Word games like Scrabble, Junior Scrabble or Boggle. Alternatively, make up your own crossword puzzles (it helps to have some photocopied blanks or squared paper on hand).

Board games. Play Monopoly or Trivial Pursuit, but first make a new set of 'chance' or question cards.

Puppet theatre. Make your own puppets (cut-outs or paper plates stuck on rulers, or glove puppets made from old socks) and create a play with them.

Cooking. Follow a recipe for a simple 'melt-and-mix' dish like chocolate crackles, or a more complicated recipe that requires cooking.

Singing. Sing your favourite add-a-verse songs, but invent new words for a change! Start with 'Old Macdonald Had a Farm' or 'She'll Be Comin' round the Mountain'.

Wherever you travel, whatever you do, have a safe and happy vacation!

CHAPTER 20
New Year's resolutions

Vivienne Nicoll

Most of us — children, parents and teachers — begin the school year with all kinds of good resolutions, and we at school would certainly like to do something special to help the children in our care. So here are some suggestions for parents which we believe will make any child's learning more effective and enjoyable. Each idea, if acted upon, will help provide a foundation at home for what we educators, your partners in education, are doing at school.

FOSTER READING IN YOUR HOME

Children are most likely to find reading purposeful and enjoyable when they see those closest to them, their family, enjoying reading and using all types of print to help them in daily living. So...
- Make a point of turning off the television sometimes and curling up on the lounge with a book instead. Talk about what you're reading, as well as asking children about their current favourites.
- Discuss items of interest from newspapers and magazines, reading snippets aloud from time to time.
- Involve children in your practical reading around the house — following a recipe, a pattern, or instructions from a manual. Don't forget all the little opportunities for showing that print is useful — the shopping list, the television guide, the telephone directory, even junk mail.
- Share letters and greeting cards with the whole family whenever possible.
- Show your children that you too find reference books useful: make a point of using dictionaries and encyclopedias in your daily life.
- Visit the municipal library together, as a family. Don't just pop in and borrow a book, but stay a while from time to time to find books or magazines to pursue a special hobby or interest.
- Give books as presents on special occasions. Make a book a birthday must!
- Establish the daily habit of reading to the children — and Dad, don't let Mum be the only one to enjoy this special before-bedtime treat.
- Encourage private reading each night before lights out.

FOSTER WRITING IN YOUR HOME

Children may see their parents as good models of reading, but often writing is something which they think happens only at school. They think that writing might be necessary for learning, but not for getting things done from day to day. So, become a writing family...

• Have fun writing messages to each other — reminders about important forthcoming events, little jokes and riddles, notes about jobs to be done. Stick them on a special board, on the fridge — wherever! Encourage the receiver of the message to write a short reply.

• Revive the lost art of letter writing. Write to friends and relations you don't see very often, and involve every member of the family in adding to the letter. Children could write to a penfriend in another state or country. Use letter writing also to comment on television programs, to express opinions, to get things done.

• Keep a family journal in which you regularly write down recounts of interesting family happenings: special days, funny incidents, holiday trips, weekend excursions and so on. Don't forget to bring the journal out and read it from time to time.

• Involve the family in writing captions for your photograph album.

• Make time on a wet weekend for word games: magazine puzzles and crosswords, or a family game of Scrabble or Boggle.

• Keep a family book of favourite poems and sayings.

• If you have to write reports for work, or essays for a course you're taking, show your children what you're doing. They will be especially interested to see that you write more than one draft, that you make changes and cross things out, and that you occasionally need to consult a dictionary for the correct spelling of a word.

• Talk with the children about the stories or other texts they have written at school. (Don't be too critical about mistakes in grammar and spelling.) Your interest will help them feel good about themselves as writers.

• Give presents which encourage writing: for younger children, an array of scrap and 'proper' paper, pencils, crayons and felt pens; for older children add notepaper and envelopes, a diary or journal, even a second-hand typewriter.

FOSTER TALKING IN YOUR HOME

• Revive the lost art of conversation. Children's fluency improves and their vocabulary grows as they converse with more mature language users. Try eating the evening meal sitting at the table, without television or radio, so that the family can share the events of the day.

• Cultivate children's curiosity. Encourage them to ask questions, to wonder about things, to have hunches...and then to check them out. Follow up their interests in nature, science, animals, the local community, television documentaries and so on.

• Discuss excursions. After school excursions, talk about the things that were seen and done. One of the most valuable results of children's outings is to be found in their use of language to relive and make sense of the experience. Sometimes the follow-up talk may lead naturally into reading and writing. You can encourage children to make a list of the most interesting things they saw or learnt, or a list of the questions they

still want answered. Perhaps now is the time to visit the library and find a relevant book, one with plenty of photographs as well as text.
• Encourage imaginative play. When children dress up or play different types of make-believe games, they are developing both their language and the creative side of their personality.

WHAT ABOUT TELEVISION?

Have a family policy that puts television firmly in its place. That box in the corner can be a wonderful servant but a monstrous master! A balanced viewing program leaves plenty of time for homework, hobbies, reading and writing, play, sport...and family conversation.

A FINAL POINT

Above all, be clear about the difference between pressure, which can destroy self-confidence and the excitement of learning; and encouragement, which stimulates growth and true achievement.

GLOSSARY

alternative spelling — see *invented spelling*

barking at print — symptom of a reading problem where the child reads out a string of unconnected words bearing little relation to the text; also called *word-calling*

brainstorming — the quick compiling or jotting down of ideas

conference — individual or small group discussion between teacher and students aimed at improving understandings in reading, literature or writing

conventional spelling — standard English spelling

conventions — aspects of spelling, grammar, punctuation and handwriting in a piece of writing

creative writing — a traditional form of fiction writing involving elements of self-expression (once called *composition)*

cursive writing — handwriting with letters joined together (a faster and more fluent style than printing, which children learn when they enter school)

DEAR — *drop everything and read* — a silent reading strategy used in the classroom

deviant spelling stage — the initial stage of spelling where young children use letters, numbers or squiggles to represent words (also call the *pre-communicative stage)*

directed writing — writing produced within a framework or specific guidelines

echo-reading — see *NIM*

edit — proofread a draft in order to improve it (involves checking spelling, grammar, punctuation, layout and sense)

enduring literacy — the level of literacy development where reading and writing are valued and used consistently for a variety of purposes

functional literacy — the standard of literacy considered to be the minimum necessary for operating in society

genre — term used to describe different forms of writing, each reflecting a different purpose (pronounced 'zhon-ra', with a soft *g* like the *s* in *measure)*

genre-based approach — a directed approach to teaching writing, aimed at teaching students to write in specific forms or genres

grammar — a system of rules describing words and their arrangement in sentences and texts

invented spelling — young children's made-up attempts to spell unknown words (also referred to as *alternative, non-standard* or *temporary spelling)*

lap-reading — shared reading, with the young child sitting on the adult's lap

modelling — indirect teaching strategy, involving performing or demonstrating a skill

NIM — the *neurological impress method* — used to help children who lack fluency in reading; also called *echo reading* (adult and child read aloud, with the adult leading and the child echoing)

non-standard spelling — see *invented spelling*

oral reading — any of a variety of forms of reading aloud

phonetic spelling — developmental stage of spelling where all the sounds in words are approximately represented

pre-phonetic spelling — early stage of spelling development, showing minimal relationship between letters and sounds

process writing — an approach to teaching writing where writers go through the process of rehearsing, drafting, revising, editing and publishing a piece

publish — to prepare a piece of writing for an audience

reading-like behaviour — actions of young non-readers, e.g. turning pages and reciting text, which indicate a developing understanding of the reading process

rehearse — to gather information and experiment with ideas before writing

retelling — a form of reading evaluation where a child tells an adult the main aspects of a story

shared book experience — shared reading, usually in the classroom with large-sized books suitable for all children to see

shared language experience — the spoken interaction between adult and child which relates to a common experience, e.g. a trip to the zoo

shared reading — reading involving interaction between adult and child (includes such aspects as reading aloud together and discussing aspects of a story)

standard spelling — conventional spelling, as found in dictionaries

temporary spelling — see *invented spelling*

text — a piece of writing

transitional spelling stage — developmental stage of spelling where the writer is aware of aspects of spelling that go beyond letter-sound relationships

USSR — *uninterrupted sustained silent reading* — a silent reading strategy used in the classroom

WEIRD — *we enjoy independent reading daily* — a silent reading strategy used in the classroom

writers' circle — term used to describe a group writing conference

Compiled by Ross Weightman

BIBLIOGRAPHY

FURTHER READING

For parents seeking further reading on aspects of their children's literacy development, we recommend the following titles:
- Reading:

Margaret Meek, *Learning to Read*, Bodley Head, 1982.
Ann Pulvertaft, *Carry on Reading*, Ashton Scholastic, 1989.
Frank Smith, *Reading*, 2nd edn, Cambridge University Press, 1985.
- 'Process' writing:

Ann Pulvertaft, *Carry on Writing*, Ashton Scholastic, 1989.
Jan Turbill, *No Better Way to Teach Writing!*, Primary English Teaching Association, 1982.
- The 'genre-based' approach:

John Collerson (ed.), *Writing for Life*, Primary English Teaching Association, 1988.
Beverly Derewianka, *Exploring How Texts Work*, Primary English Teaching Association, 1990.
- Spelling:

Wendy Bean & Chrystine Bouffler, *Spell by Writing*, Primary English Teaching Association, 1987.
Richard Gentry, *Spel is a Four-Letter Word*, Scholastic, 1987.
- Literacy in action:

Hazel Brown & Vonne Mathie, *Inside Whole Language: A Classroom View*, Primary English Teaching Association, 1990.
Brian Cambourne, *The Whole Story: Natural Learning and the Acquisition of Literacy in the Classroom*, Ashton Scholastic, 1988.
Frank Smith, *Joining the Literacy Club*, Heinemann, 1988.

USEFUL BOOK GUIDES FOR PARENTS

Belle Alderman, *The Ashton Scholastic Guide to Best Books for Children*, Ashton Scholastic, 1989.
Dorothy Butler, *Babies Need Books: How to Share the Joy of Reading with Your Child*, Penguin Books, 1987.
Dorothy Butler, *Five to Eight*, Bodley Head, 1987.
Walter McVitty, *The PETA Guide to Children's Literature*, 2nd edn, Primary English Teaching Association, 1989.
Maurice Saxby & Glenys Smith, *First Choice: A Guide to Best Books for Children*, Oxford University Press, 1991.
Jim Trelease, *The Read-Aloud Handbook*, Penguin Books, 1987.

OTHER PETA PUBLICATIONS FOR PARENTS

Barry Dwyer, *Parents Teachers Partners*, 1989.
Barry Dwyer and others, *A Letter to Parents*, Pen 7 (pamphlet).
Barry Dwyer, *Today's Child at School: A Parent's Guide*, PEN 62 (pamphlet).
Barry Dwyer, *Parents' Guide to the 'Basics'* (brochure).